Benchmarking
A Life in Business

"TODO SE PUEDE"

Benchmarking
A Life in Business
"*Todo se puede*"

BY BURT CABAÑAS

My thanks to Sally E. DiPaula, who has done such a fine job helping me to put my thoughts into words.

Copyright © 2014 by **Hawthorn Creative**

All rights reserved. No part of this book may be reproduced in any form without written permission of the copyright owners. All images in this book have been reproduced with the knowledge and prior consent of the artists concerned and no responsibility is accepted by the producer, publisher, or printer for any infringement of copyright or otherwise arising from the contents of this publication. Every effort has been made to ensure that credits accurately comply with information supplied.

First published in the United States of America by
Hawthorn Creative.

33 Jewell Court
Portsmouth, New Hampshire 03801

Telephone: 603-610-0533

Fax: 603-610-0532

HAWTHORNCREATIVE.COM

This book is dedicated to my mother, Elena Cabañas. As you read this book, it will be clear that my mother's approach to life, "*todo se puede*," has been the major influence in my life since I was 10 years old.

And, of course, to my wife, Hermys, who, for 40 years has made all of my successes possible. There are no words to express my appreciation for her and all she has done for me and our children, Kaira and Alex.

Table of Contents

Foreword	9
Preface	15
From Cuba to The Woodlands	21
Be the Difference	29
Listening Beats Talking	39
Taking Risks	51
Check Your Ego at the Door	63
Let It Take Its Course	73
Unexpected Gestures	81
Can You Live with It for the Rest of Your Life?	89
Mosaic	99
Todo Se Puede	107
Afterword	119

Foreword

By David Gottlieb, PhD

Burt Cabañas and I have known one another and worked together for more than 25 years. I was running conferences at The Woodlands Conference Center back in the early 1980s when Burt became the vice president and general manager there. And thank goodness he did. That property had been inappropriately positioned and had been losing money for four years. Burt turned the entire operation around and made it into one of the top 10 conference centers in the United States. Clearly, Burt learned to lead at a young age.

Burt and I have always gotten along well, perhaps because we have something important in common: our immigrant background. He came to this country from Cuba as a very young boy, and my parents came here as Jewish immigrants escaping the violence of the Russian revolution in Belarus. One special memory relating to that background goes back to a conversation I had with George Mitchell, chairman and CEO of Mitchell

Energy and Development Corporation, whose own father was the son of a Greek immigrant who came to Galveston, Texas as a day laborer who laid railroad tracks. I had asked George a very blunt question: "Why do you want to continue employing me even though I have no experience in the energy field or in land development?" (At the time, I was serving as the dean of the College of Social Sciences at the University of Houston.) I will never forget his response: He said he had an abundance of

| George Mitchell, Chairman & CEO, Mitchell Energy and Development.

well-credentialed engineers, architects, accountants, and attorneys; what he was looking for were more people like himself—smart, hard-working, determined people not born into wealth or an entitlement. He wanted folks who had to travel a non-conventional path in order to achieve their goals and fulfill their dreams. And then he said, "Burt Cabañas is an excellent example of this type of person."

Burt started working almost immediately after arriving in Florida from Cuba. A Spanish-speaking kid with limited family resources, he set goals he was determined to reach. He was going to learn English, be a support to his mother and sister, do well in school, work hard at any job he could get—even pool boy and lifeguard—and one day found his own company.

Part of the reason why Burt has been so successful is that he has always been looking forward. In early 1980, he was one of the first people to recognize that the demographics of resorts, hotels, and conference centers were changing significantly and that more and more women would be attending all kinds of meetings and events, but the hospitality industry was not focused on them. Burt understood that women needed enhanced security, certain kinds of amenities in the rooms, certain types of food to be served.

He also was one of the first leaders to understand that international companies were increasing their presence in the United States both in investment in real estate and in the use of conference centers. In 1992, he asked me to travel with him to Tokyo and accompany him to his meetings with developers and banks there. My job was to explain the culture and the specific business practices that were unique to Japan. Burt was focused on how to approach this new market.

Then as today, I saw the passion, initiative, and intuitive ability of Burt and knew that he would learn the financial, political, and organizational skills needed to succeed at the highest levels in business. And I was right. Burt learned his lessons very well. He was wise enough to recruit, hire, and educate outstanding employees and design a corporate culture and a hospitality organization that has not only survived the various economic and political storms of the past 30 years, but has flourished and grown, both domestically and internationally.

How Burt pulled off the creation and development of a unique hospitality management company and managed to survive through several US and world economic and political crises will become clear as you read this book. He was never afraid, he learned from his mistakes, and he recruited and hired the best people, whom he trusted and empowered.

But to me, what is more important about Burt, and something I know first-hand, is that he is a warm, compassionate man who holds to his principles. I think this quote from Thomas Jefferson describes Burt perfectly: "In matters of fashion I swim with the stream—in matters of principle I stand like a rock."

Burt's origins taught him that many people face problems and difficulties and have to struggle to make it. He saw his mother face adversity and hardship, and successfully overcome them. And now he is sharing with us much of what he has learned in his many years at Benchmark. I am sure you will be glad he decided to do so.

Preface

For more than 30 years, I have had the pleasure of telling stories about Benchmark's employees, customers, partners, and suppliers at meetings and events. And when appropriate, I would reflect on some of the business philosophies that have guided our company from its beginnings. Since people were always generous when listening to what I had to say, I was able to refine my thinking on a number of these principles. However, since I do not consider myself a writer, these stories and principles have remained oral for the most part.

Over the last couple of years, two people—Ellen Sinclair, Benchmark senior vice president; and my son, Alex, today Benchmark's chief executive officer—told me that although those who work most closely with me benefit from these stories and principles, Benchmark was now too large to expect word of mouth alone to share them with our employees. Because of this and because Alex and Ellen believed strongly that I should share my story and my business philosophy more broadly, they pressed me to write it all down. Alex was especially persuasive in this regard. "These principles now belong to all of us, not just to you," he told me.

So, in this book, I am sharing these philosophies, these core principles that have not only shaped my life and my career, but have become the foundation of Benchmark Hospitality International. These are principles that have served me for my whole life and have made it possible for me to grow a company that today has more than 6,000 employees—employees who create memorable moments for the guests of resorts, conference centers, and hotels. Just as important, these are the principles that helped me to grow from a recently arrived, Cuban-American kid in school in Miami Beach, to beach clean-up boy as my first real job, to the founder and chairman of Benchmark Hospitality International.

To every employee who reads this book, I hope you enjoy this compilation of the leadership principles that form the bedrock of our company. I will be pleased if it proves helpful as you strive to achieve your goals and dreams.

Benchmarking
A Life in Business

"TODO SE PUEDE"

From Cuba to The Woodlands

It all started in Cuba. One of my earliest memories as a child is of my father dying of cancer when I was 7 years old, leaving my mother, Elena, to raise and support my younger sister, Maria Elena, and me. It was a tough situation to be in, but my mother coped with it and coped well. She moved to Miami, found a place to live and got a job. For about a year, Maria Elena and I stayed in Cuba with my godmother and grandfather before joining my mother in Miami, where she was working as a beautician.

So there we were, in a foreign country, with very little money and even less English.

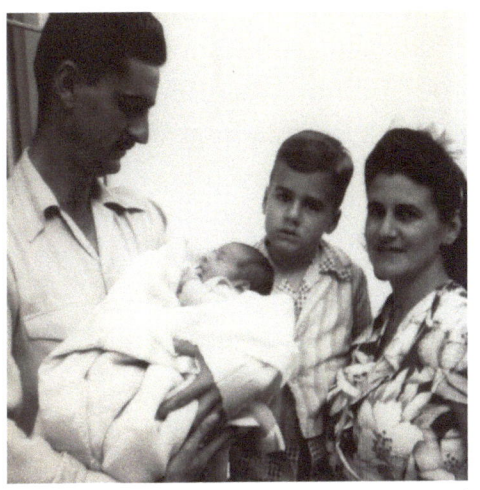

My father with my newborn sister, Maria Elena, my mother, and me.

In those days, my mother thought, and so did I, that we would return to Cuba in a year or two and resume ours lives there, though without my father. But that didn't happen. In late 1959, Castro came to power in Cuba and, by the early 1960s, when other families left Cuba, we knew we were not going back soon.

During that time, I was in the local elementary school, repeating the fourth grade because of my poor English. But kids adapt fast, and in six months I had learned English and was working hard to fit in. Sports helped me make friends quickly.

Of course, if you've lost your father and then moved to another country and are surviving on very little money, you have to be sure to keep your head down and keep moving forward. And that's what my sister, Maria, and I did. But in one very important way, we were lucky. We had our mother there to remind us of the way forward. If one of us would complain about some difficulty or obstacle, she would look at us and say, *"Todo se puede!"* That was her constant message to us. "Everything is possible" or "You can do it." I like to think that following this advice as an immigrant and then an exile in this country added another booster to my engine and is probably the reason why challenges always get my adrenaline going.

What she meant, of course, is that if you are determined and willing to work hard, you can achieve your goals. Even today, I live this principle. Everyone at Benchmark has come to understand this: "It may seem difficult at first, but you can do it if you give it your time, effort, energy, and resources." And the history of our company proves how on target this principle is.

That is why, when new employees join Benchmark, we let them know that they can be successful if they have the right attitude, are willing to work hard, and are determined to meet their goals. And we have many employees who have done just that. As a matter of fact, one-third of Benchmark's management team got their start in the company as hourly employees, working the front desk or washing pots and pans or maybe even serving as pool boys or girls. We take pride in this fact.

Let me give you an example. Mike Van Duzer started with us right out of school as a conference services attendant at the Resort at Squaw Creek, setting up tables and chairs for events. Within a year, he was promoted to utility engineer in the maintenance department. Then another promotion, this time to duty engineer, took him to Lansdowne Resort, where his strong performance brought him to the attention of the Cheyenne Mountain Resort team. They lured Mike away to become their director of facilities. Today, Mike serves as director of facilities at Deloitte University, an 800-guest-room hotel and conference center built by Deloitte as its center for leadership development, where he manages a team of 23. And despite carrying this obviously serious workload for our company, he still finds time for his wife and three children and for his community, working for a prison ministry and the Boys and Girls Club of America, and helping the elderly in his community's care centers. Mike came this far because of his hard work and his skills—but most of all, because of his determination, his belief that everything is possible.

Of course, during the almost 30 years between my arrival in Miami as a non-English-speaking child and my purchase of Benchmark with its employees like Mike, a lot happened. I worked through junior high and high school, starting at the age of 12 delivering papers, then cleaning the swimming pool at the Shelborne Hotel. For four years, I would go to the hotel

Kaira, Hermys, and Alex.

right after school and work until sundown. After that, I joined the Marine Corps Reserves, served my active duty requirement and returned to the hotel industry. During this time, I started and continued my college studies. Along the way, early in my career, I married Hermys Rodriguez and had two children, my daughter, Kaira, and my son, Alex (now president and chief executive officer of Benchmark Hospitality).

Twenty-five years into my career, I bought the Benchmark Management Company.

This is how it happened. I had been working with Mitchell Energy & Development Corporation's real estate development subsidiary, The Woodlands Corporation, since 1979. My challenge was to turn around the financial performance of The Woodlands Resort and Conference Center; it had lost more than $4 million in its first five years of existence. It was a difficult challenge to meet, but two years later, the resort and conference center was completely out of the red and had turned a $2.5 million profit in 1982.

Over time, though, I came to believe that a small subsidiary in a very large company was not the best place to be. Long-term compensation programs for key managers, for instance, were geared toward rewarding success in oil and gas exploration or real estate development, not necessarily toward the profitable contributions to the operation of the hospitality management company. So in early 1985, I approached George Mitchell about structuring an incentive for the key people in Benchmark based on their specific success, one that was not tied to oil and gas stock or land development stock. I personally was prepared to give up the 12,000 shares in Mitchell Energy I had earned as senior vice president of The Woodlands Corporation to get this accomplished.

After many levels of discussion, Mr. Mitchell decided to sell the hospitality management company to me and maintain an arm's-length relationship. I gave up my Mitchell Energy stock and established incentives for individuals based on Benchmark's performance. Later, he remarked that he sold me the company because he knew I could do a better job running it than The Woodlands Corporation could. And that was how what was then known as the Benchmark Management Company and now as Benchmark Hospitality International came into being.

I had to sign three notes: one was for the value of the company on the day of purchase; one was for a residual participation that The Woodlands Corporation would retain for any new deals that came into the company for a period of 10 years; and the third was a 90-day note that replaced the operating capital in the company. It was difficult raising the money for that 90-day note. I had to mortgage everything: my kids' college funds, our home, everything. But 90 days later, I was able to repay that note. Somehow, after many sleepless nights, I got it done.

The notes I signed, coupled with the reduction in fee

revenue from The Woodlands Resort and Conference Center, amounted to just over $2,800,000 over the next 10-year period, an amount that might seem small today in terms of buying a company, but back then, it was a significant amount of money. Up to that point, I had never earned more than $65,000 in salary in a year. You can believe this was a very big commitment to me. I was 39 years old with a wife and two children to support. But I took the risk.

And every day that I worked to pay off those notes, one thought stayed in my mind: my mother's advice that everything is possible. If I hadn't believed that, I never would have put my livelihood—and that of my family—on the line to make this purchase.

We began by having five conference centers under contract: The Woodlands Resort and Conference Center in Texas; the San Luis Resort in Galveston, Texas; The Cottages on Hilton Head Island, South Carolina; Chaminade in Santa Cruz, California; and Cheyenne Mountain Inn in Colorado Springs, Colorado. To this day, we still operate the last two.

Throughout my career, I have followed my mother's core belief that everything is possible, yet it is only one of many principles and practices that have guided my business decisions since my teenage job as a beach clean-up boy in Miami Beach. There are many others, and in this book I would like to share them with you with the goal of encouraging you to think about them in relation to your own career with the hope that they might help you create the future you envision for yourself.

Be the Difference

Being a man or a woman is a matter of birth. Being a man or a woman who makes a difference is a matter of choice. -Byron Garrett

Many of our nation's most important and influential companies find a way to communicate their company culture through a simple statement of purpose or philosophy. Consider the following mottos that are so familiar to us: Nike—"Just do it"; Southwest Airlines—"If it matters to you, it matters to us"; IBM—"Think." Many institutions also explain themselves in this way: Johns Hopkins University—"The truth will set you free." And one I fondly remember from my youth and the United States Marines—"Semper Fidelis" (Always Faithful).

In this same vein, once Benchmark had grown to more than 6,000 employees, we knew it was time for us to find an effective way to describe our culture, a way that would be clear and useful and would capture the essence of what our employees strive to do every day. Of course, like other successful companies, years back, we had codified the core values of the company, as well as our key service priorities, and these values and priorities form the foundation of the Benchmark culture. And we are proud of the fact that this foundation came from the bottom up; that is, it was built by our staff, not created at the executive level and pushed down through the organization. But, like IBM and other corporations, we needed a key phrase that would sum up Benchmark and explain to those outside the company—investors, customers, clients, vendors, and prospective employees—what sets us apart in the hospitality industry.

As we worked to come up with this phrase, we realized that there were a lot of good things to say about our company: our entrepreneurship, our unique group of properties, our family culture, our "Mosaic" of technical and interpersonal skills, and so on.

After giving it a great deal of thought, our leadership team realized that the best approach was an obvious one that echoes what I talk about in the next chapter: Ask our employees what they value about the work they do, listen to their answers, and go from there. So that's what we did.

We had the general managers of our properties ask the employees why they enjoy their work and what gives them job satisfaction. Among the feedback we got—and there was a lot of it—one response came up again and again: "I make a difference in the lives of people who come through our doors, and I make a difference in the lives of the employees who work with me." Over and over, our employees told us that being the difference was the reason they found job satisfaction day in, day out.

Thank goodness we started by listening to our employees

and avoided imposing a Home Office-generated catchphrase because we ended up with the three most important words in the company and a superb summary of what Benchmark is all about: Be the Difference. And, fortunately, since it was already happening, all we needed to do was describe it, celebrate it, and let it take its course.

Now, from a Home Office perspective, we view our job as making it as easy as possible for our employees to make a difference, small or large, to give them the opportunity to be themselves in their work and in their interactions with the guests, the freedom to think and do things on their own. We see the fruits of this every day, an employee taking the initiative to help a guest or make a guest's stay more comfortable or fun or welcoming.

Take, for example, Benchmark housekeepers in Hawaii, who make little animals out of the towels for all the children who stay with us. There was never a policy for making animal toys out of towels; the housekeepers decided to do it on their own. This same sense of initiative is found at the Bardessono, where two doormen—Kyle Christian and Aaron Gordon—took the initiative to replace a bottle of special wine a guest had broken as she got out of her car in front of the hotel.

The way I see it, giving our employees the freedom to think and act on their own not only makes a difference in the lives of our guests, but also creates the very success our company has had. We have never been a one-size-fits-all company, and encouraging our employees to think and act on their own ensures that we don't operate one-size-fits-all hotels and resorts and conference centers.

One reason I know this is from the messages guests send

to us week after week:

> In all my years of traveling, I have never encountered anyone who catered to my needs as much as Eyob did; he took ownership of my problem and obviously had the freedom to make a decision to put my mind at ease. It was world class all the way.

This guest was late for a flight, and Eyob Vasquez, knowing the guest had to get home to her family, promised that he would get her to the airport on time. And he made another promise: "In case we don't make it on time to check your bag, I will take it back to the hotel and ship it to you tomorrow." Now Eyob had committed himself to a lot of work and to shipping the luggage to a distant location, none of which is a normal part of his job. But this attitude—"we are going to help this guest no matter what"—is what sets Benchmark service apart. And it felt good learning that our guest appreciated the fact that Eyob was free to make a difference without having to clear it with his boss.

Not only is "Be the

THE EXTRA MILE

Consider the story of the surgical equipment marketing rep who was dropping something off at The Chattanoogan. She had just arrived in the public parking area when three police cars and a SWAT van blocked her car, and one officer warned her that she was going to be there for quite a while. The rep had to be at a downtown restaurant to make a presentation to a group of surgeons, and everything she needed for it was in her car. In her own words, as she was holding back tears, "If I don't show up, I'll be toast."

And here is where Kyle Petty from Valet was the difference. He immediately grabbed one of the center's vans, loaded everything the sales rep needed for the presentation from her car into it, drove her to the restaurant, and helped her carry her equipment inside. When the rep returned to the hotel after her presentation, her car was waiting for her at Valet. Fortunately, Kyle wasn't concerned about the fact that the rep was not a guest at our property; he was concerned with her situation and how to resolve it. He wanted to fix the problem, not just get rid of it. In short, he wanted to "Be the Difference."

Difference" the right thing to do for our customers, but it is also good for the owners of the properties we manage and for our clients. The value to the owners of the properties we manage is that they partner with a company whose employees treat each property as if they owned it, and they treat the guests the way an owner would.

I often remind the Benchmark team how powerful and long-lasting a "Be the Difference" gesture to a guest can be. Sometimes, we are talking about years. When Mike Taylor was serving as general manager at the North Maple Inn in New Jersey, he was called down to the front desk by a woman who had asked for him specifically. She introduced herself and asked if Mike remembered her name. He didn't. This is what she told him:

> *Well, I know your name very well because more than two years ago, my husband lost a winter coat here. He wasn't sure where he lost it, but he was hoping your housekeeping staff would come across it. They never did find the jacket. Apparently, my husband had told you how important it was for him to find it because I had just given it to him as a Christmas present. He was pretty upset with himself, but you saved the day. You found exactly the same kind of jacket and had it shipped to us. We were amazed at such customer service.*

She went on to tell Mike that her husband made her promise that the next time she had to organize a meeting in the area, she would use the North Maple Inn because he knew, first-hand, how well the place is run.

But it's really not so important that she ended up bringing a group to the conference center. Though that was generous of her, what's important for us at Benchmark is to remember how much our guests appreciate the efforts we make on their behalf, sometimes remembering them for years after the fact.

I've already mentioned that we are not a one-size-fits-all operation. This is what gives each of the properties we manage its own personality and saves us from the homogeneity we often find with some of the national hotel chains. In delivering service, our employees can be not only engaged but creative.

One of my favorite examples of this involved my wife, Hermys. We were in Miami, and Hermys saw a sad news report on the local TV station about a serious crime that had occurred at a Miami Beach resort at the same time that a wedding reception was taking place there. Since the police evacuated the hotel, the couple and their guests had to abruptly cut short the reception. Hermys saw the couple being interviewed on a local TV station. During the interview, they mentioned that they were on their way to our Turtle Bay Resort for their honeymoon. So, Hermys had me call Turtle Bay just to let them know the honeymooners' situation. I didn't make any suggestions to the staff about how to treat the couple; I just let them know what had happened. And here is where the staff showed both their thoughtfulness and

Hermys and me at home.

creativity: They re-created a wedding reception—cake, music, and leis included—and surprised the couple with it. And since the original guests weren't available, staff members took their place, toasting and congratulating the newlyweds.

As I mentioned in the beginning of this chapter, "Be the Difference" doesn't apply only to guests; it also applies to Benchmark employees who are committed to their coworkers. Recently, an employee in the housekeeping department at the Snow King Resort was diagnosed with a serious medical condition that required immediate surgery. On the eve of the surgery, four of her fellow employees traveled 139 miles one way to visit her in the hospital—after they had all worked their normal day. And they carried with them a bag of "well wishes," which included the patient's name tag, coffee mug, paycheck, a paid-time-off request form, and—to supply her with all the comforts of her housekeeping department—shampoo, lotion, a roll of toilet paper, rubber gloves, cleaning rags, a spray bottle, and garbage bags.

There are even cases when our guests are so kind and generous that they teach us how to make a difference. The Inn at Virginia Tech provides an example of this in a good-news, bad-news, good-news story.

The good news was that Tabatha Hughes, a room attendant, gave birth via C-section to

PLUS ONE
Creative thinking–along with determination to solve a customer's problem–came into play at the Eaglewood Resort and Spa, where Lisa and Jim were about to get married. The day before the wedding, Lisa's father was taken to the hospital. There was talk of canceling the wedding, but the couple and their families decided that the ceremony must go on. That's when Eric Pluff and Rick Franzen on the resort's event staff got creative. Working with the hospital, they set up a Skype call between Lisa's father and the wedding party. As a result, the father of the bride was "present" not only for the wedding itself, but also for the dinner and dancing that followed.

an eight-pound baby boy. Then the bad news: While Tabatha was still in the hospital, her rented home burned to the ground. Fortunately, no one was there at the time, so there were no injuries, but the house was a total loss. And now some more good news: The University of Maryland Women's Basketball Team happened to be staying at the inn for a game. One of the players was in the service elevator on her way to the Fitness Center when she saw an internal notice to the staff reporting on the incident. She told her teammates, and when they checked out on Sunday, they left a donation of $282 in cash for Tabatha and her family and some extra clothes, as did some of the staff at the inn who read the notice. Though the money must have been of help to Tabatha, think of what a difference it made knowing that even total strangers were concerned with her well-being.

I could go on for pages about the many thoughtful acts and gestures, both large and small, that our employees make every day. It might be cutting up a steak for a customer whose arm is in a cast or purchasing groceries for a financially strapped coworker or buying a board game for a guest's child who is too sick to enjoy the Florida sun. Or—back to weddings—it might be finding the perfect location for a guest to propose to his fiancée. Wherever and whenever, Benchmark employees are committed to being the difference for others. The stories we share around the company, like the ones in this chapter, are the lifeblood of Benchmark, and they inspire me every day, even after having been in this business since I was 15 years old.

Though all of us must go to work every day to earn a living and support our loved ones, Benchmark employees also enjoy serving others who are away from their homes and often under stress from their own work and responsibilities. When one of our team makes a difference to a guest, it affirms our desire to be in the hospitality business. We are fortunate that our business lives enable us to support and help those who have placed their trust in our professionalism by staying at a Benchmark resort or hotel.

As to the effect this philosophy has on the employees themselves, I think one of them said it best when he described his adjustment to our "Be the Difference" culture.

> *All I did to set the wheel in motion was to decide to change my outlook on life once and for all and commit to it. Not for a day, not for a month, but for good. Then, I took small steps. I said yes instead of saying no. I smiled instead of frowning. I complimented instead of criticizing. I gave positivity and I got positivity in return. I couldn't believe it worked, but it was evident that I was a happier, more fulfilled person.*

Of all the factors that contribute to Benchmark's success, there is none more important than our employees' willingness to confront whatever problem they encounter and take risks for the sake of others. To support these efforts, all of us in leadership positions make it clear that there is not just one way, one procedure, or one approach to each situation in our business. Rather, our employees are encouraged to "chameleon themselves" to their individual property and then do what it takes to make that property successful. Our deep belief in encouraging employees to be themselves and to think creatively is the bedrock of Benchmark and central to the guest experience at each of our properties. That's why we summed it up in three words: "Be the Difference."

Listening Beats Talking

We have two ears and one mouth so that we can listen twice as much as we speak. -Epictetus

I admit that this advice is often hard to follow. First, listening is difficult to do well. Most of us have to make a real effort to slow down and listen carefully to what a spouse, friend, or co-worker is saying to us. Second, daily life can be demanding and distracting, so we tend to focus on our own needs rather than on those around us. Nevertheless, to listen well is not only good advice, but also perhaps the best advice I can give you.

The importance of listening is something I learned when very young, in fact, beginning the day I first arrived in this country, getting off the plane in my Hopalong Cassidy

My mother with Maria and me in our Hopalong Cassidy costumes.

outfit. As I wrote earlier, Spanish was my first and, at that time, my only language. Suddenly, I found myself in a country where everyone spoke English. As hard as it is to believe now, in the early 1950s, there were very few Cubans in Miami. In fact, the predominant population consisted of people who had moved down from the North to avoid the cold or to retire. So, on my first day of school, what I found was a teacher and students who not only didn't speak Spanish but who expected me to speak English. So for the first few years in my American school, I listened and listened hard—twice as hard as anybody else—just to make sure I understood what they were saying to me.

Later, as a young adult, I was lucky enough to work with several people who, by their actions, showed me how important listening is. One of my models for good listening was Arnold Seamon, the vice president of the Doral Resort and Golf Club. I worked there as a conference service manager, night manager, director of international sales, and director of operations. Arnold never forgot what anybody said in a meeting, and he always took notes. To this day, he still has pads of paper on his desk with information and tasks he has to address and with whom.

The necessity to listen intently to learn English and the role modeling I received in my first "grown-up" jobs are just two reasons why, over the years, I've tried to create an environment of listening here at Benchmark. And that's why we put in place 1-866-My-Culture. Every call that comes into this 24-hour hotline is transcribed and given directly to Alex and me. The number is real, and it is a quick way for any Benchmark employee to bring a compliment, complaint, problem, or recommendation to our attention.

And employees do call. There are calls that relate to the organization, that is, about company policies or procedures and about how we handle certain benefits or programs. These calls are relatively easy to handle, so we make sure the employee gets a response as quickly as possible.

But there are also calls with complaints about supervisors or complaints relating to promotions or performance reviews and the like. We investigate every one of these. After all, whether the complaint turns out to be actionable or not, it is very real to our employees or they wouldn't have taken the time to call us. So we owe it to them to listen and to follow up. And we do. It should also be said that we receive compliments about supervisors who have earned the respect of their team.

To handle some issues, we need time to conduct research or interview people. When that's the case, we contact the employee by phone or e-mail to let him or her know we are working on the issue or complaint. And if we believe that a vice president, a regional manager, or supervisor may be somehow involved or their objectivity compromised, we find a person from another area to address the problem. What's important to me is that we don't soften the issue but pursue it with a sense of urgency because it's our ethical and fiduciary responsibility to do so.

Sadly, we even get calls asking for help with personal problems such as lack of money or difficulties at home. In these cases, though we normally can't intervene, we make sure that the person feels heard and that we express our concern for their struggles.

This has been my approach at Benchmark from the beginning. It actually goes back to the years before I purchased the company from George Mitchell, when I was general manager at The Woodlands Resort. When I arrived on the scene, there were a considerable number of problems, and the resort and conference center was losing money. One of the first steps I took was to install a red phone in my home, a direct line from The Woodlands's switchboard. (Can you believe that we had switchboards in those days?) Anyone could call me, at any time of day. There were lots of calls because, as I mentioned, there were lots of issues to address.

As you can imagine, the timing of the calls was not always convenient, and the problems were not always easy to solve. But we were able to solve most of them, largely because we listened and identified the scope of each problem. I installed this hotline because, if employees lack a voice in the organization or if their supervisors do not listen to them, the employees will cease to be the difference that sets a resort and conference center and our team apart.

At the same time that we set up the hotline, I started listening carefully to the management team of The Woodlands. One Tuesday morning, I gathered the top 10 or 12 managers for a meeting so I could ask them a key question: "What one thing keeps you from doing your job exactly right?" They gave all kinds of answers from "I can't get my supplies on time" to "The ownership won't let us cut the grass on a regular schedule." At first, all I did was listen. Then I wrote all their input on a flip chart and said, "From now on, what's on this flip chart is my job description. Don't worry yourselves about these issues anymore. They're my responsibility now. You just focus on your responsibilities and getting the job done."

This step took away the excuses that could be given for underperformance. And the managers responded well—so much so that the center was put on the right track in year one; at the end of year two, we turned a profit. For me, this outcome once again confirmed my view of business: The way to run an enterprise is not from the top down but from the bottom up. And to do that, you have to listen to your employees every day.

Speaking of bottom up, since Benchmark operates such a diverse portfolio of properties today, our most intense and important listening must be done at each property. As a company, we encourage each general manager to ask his or her employees about what they see, what they think, and what they recommend we do for the business. As you might expect, the employees at every level have great ideas.

Recently, Tom Cupo, one of our managing directors, held a meeting of several directors of sales and marketing. Tom wanted to hear their ideas on different ways to drive sales. He took the time and made the effort to listen to what they had to say, and this is what he learned. During the meeting, one director asked the group why they didn't cross-advertise in the monthly digital newsletters each property put out to its customer base. No one had thought of doing this. Tom thought it would work and encouraged them to try it. So, the Stonewall Resort placed an ad in the Virginia Tech Conference Center's newsletter, offering a special deal to The Inn at Virginia Tech's alumni. To track the results, the alumni were provided with a special code to use for reservations. It worked: The ad brought in $20,000 in bookings in just two months—another clear example of listening paying off, literally!

Sometimes, listening can take the form of observing, listening with our eyes. Hometown Hospitality, one of the most important programs we have instituted at Benchmark, is a case in point. Almost from the beginning days of the company, groups of employees at our properties were volunteering their time to support local organizations and events, and doing it in a wide variety of ways. At some point, we realized that it would be a good idea to establish a company-wide program for engaging the local communities in which we operate. It was originally the idea of Jim Bullock, then a vice president in sales and marketing, who took what local employees were already doing and formalized it, creating a logo and the story. That's how Hometown Hospitality became our most important community program.

When we asked the employees what community effort should be implemented first across properties, the consensus was clear: literacy programs. And this turned out to be the perfect umbrella for a range of activities that could be tailored to the needs of each locality: Some employees read to seniors with vision problems; some tutored children in reading; some taught English as a second language; some collected books for their local libraries. Because the employees believed in what they were doing, there was a lot of enthusiasm, and this enthusiasm led to success and recognition in our communities.

A Hometown Hospitality team at work for Habitat for Humanity.

Every year since, we've continued this practice. We've been involved with Habitat for Humanity, the Girls and Boys Clubs of America, and, for the last three years, the USO because the military is so important not only to us as a country, but to so many of our employees who have relatives and friends serving. As in all our Hometown Hospitality initiatives, each property selects its own way to implement a USO project by, for instance, packing Girl Scout cookies to mail to soldiers in Afghanistan or serving Thanksgiving dinner to troops in transit at the airport. And I'm proud to say that almost 80 percent of their efforts involve personal labor and time, not financial contributions.

As important as it is to listen to our employees, it is equally important to listen to our customers. When we learn what they want and need, the results can be satisfying and rewarding.

In late 2013, one of our sales managers got a call from a meeting planner for a national health group that was looking for a site for their board of directors meeting. During that call, the meeting planner emphasized how important health and wellness and healthy cuisine were to the group. Often, in such a situation, a sales team's response would be to tell the caller what we offer, write up a contract, make some minor tweaks, and present the contract to the potential client. But in this case, the sales manager was listening very carefully, and when the meeting planner arrived for a stay to test out the center, instead of placing a generic amenity such as a welcome fruit basket in her room, the team delivered a health- and wellness-related amenity. When the planner arrived at the spa, its director was on hand to walk her through the spa experience. When the sales manager took her to lunch, the chef came out to greet her and described the center's farm-to-table program, organic cuisine, and made-from-scratch meals. The planner was overwhelmed by the fact that the center's staff had listened to her so closely. Before she had arrived for her visit, she had made appointments with two of our strong competitors to see what they had to offer. But she canceled those appointments, telling the sales manager, "I really don't need to go anywhere else because you listened to what I was saying and are going to give us just what we want."

Another important way for us to listen to our customers is through formal customer feedback. Most of our properties hold a meeting every week to review all the guest feedback. This kind of organized review of customer input is really a form of listening and can be very powerful because if we get complaints, we know we need to take action.

At one of our larger properties, the team received a number of comments about the awkward positioning of the lighting system in the sleeping rooms. The light switch was next to the door. When the guests came into the room, this worked well; they could turn on all the lights right at the door with one touch of the button. However, when it was time to go to sleep, the guests had to get out of bed, walk to the switch, turn the light off, then get back in bed in the dark. It was truly awkward, so it was no surprise that there were complaints. To see what could be done about the problem, the center's director of engineering went to the manufacturer of the system. Fortunately, they had a fix: a wireless device that sits at the bedside and "speaks" to the thermostat and to the main control board, that is, the brains of the room. Problem solved. But then we thought, "If we're going to add this device to each room, why not make the most of it? Wouldn't it be nice to let the guest control not only the lights, but also the room temperature and the reading lamps individually?" And, yes, the manufacturer was able to provide a model that could do all that. The testing phase went well, and two months later, a new system was installed in every room.

What was most satisfying about this effort was the feedback the center received from many of its regular customers, who said they not only liked the new system but they appreciated the fact that the center's team listened and took action.

Just as it is with employees and guests, listening is a core responsibility in our relationships with Benchmark's property owners and directors. It's important to listen carefully not just about strategic issues, but also about tactical matters. This happened a while back when an advisory board member from one of our conference centers asked the general manager if he'd like to hear about a practice he found valuable at a hotel where he had recently stayed. Apparently, the board member had given the hotel a very high rating on the customer feedback form he had filled out. Later, he received a personal note (via e-mail) thanking him for taking the time to provide his input and suggesting that he pass on his thoughts to the TripAdvisor™ website. The note included a link to the site, making the additional effort as easy as possible.

The general manager listened to the board member's suggestion and acted on it. The conference center started sending personal notes to all guests who scored their experience at the property very highly, asking them to comment on TripAdvisor™. As a result, within a few months, the conference center moved from TripAdvisor's™ number-seven to number-one-rated property in the region.

This listening scenario plays out all the time at the Home Office and at our properties. There are things that property leaders discuss with their teams in planning meetings that do not appear to have a lot of relevance at the time. But they often show up later in some other form or stated in a new way and end up helping the business. To put it simply, if we're going to find those nuggets that enhance the business and our relationships, we have to be willing to listen to some rambling asides and wayward topics.

One of the most important examples of careful listening relates to my own office, and it comes in the form of Rita McClure, Benchmark's vice president of administration. From her first day on the job, Rita and her listening skills have made my work so much easier.

Rita answers most of the calls that come into my office. And from the caller, she finds out why the person is calling and what he/she needs. Is it a client? A sales person? A property owner? An employee? Someone looking to sell something? This is not an easy task. Many callers are not forthcoming. But Rita has always been able to listen to them in a way that is polite and convinces them that she's trying to be of help. In the earliest days of the company, I made Rita a part of Benchmark's management team, so she knows what is happening across the company, why it's happening, and how it's happening. She even knows what isn't happening that should be.

And Rita's listening and questioning skills not only save me a great deal of duplication, but they also bring another benefit: She often serves as a sounding board for me. If I want to do such and such, she asks me key questions: "What if this happens?" or "Have you thought about X?" or "Are we sure that's true?" Her listening and her probing questions help me further evaluate my thinking. And she gives me information that I may not have had otherwise.

Listening Beats Talking

As a result of her strong listening skills and her superb ability to interact with people at every level, anyone who calls my office and knows Rita is just as happy to talk to her as to me. They know that Rita will clarify the issue, take the action needed, and resolve the issue with a high level of trust.

No one of us has all the answers or all the good ideas. Therefore, this simple principle of careful listening will remain one of the key elements of Benchmark culture. We will stick with this important behavior: Be open to listening, listen, take action, then start listening again to the other person, whoever it is—an employee, a customer, or an owner. Make no mistake, careful listening is hard; it is taxing, and it requires a lot of effort. But it is always the right thing to do.

Taking Risks

Only those who will risk going too far can possibly find out how far one can go. -T. S. Eliot

In some companies, risks may be viewed as fatal. Fast-track employees, those marked for success, know they had better work cautiously and avoid risky decisions if they want to move ahead. This is not the case at Benchmark. Here, we know that the highest achievement happens when an employee takes risks—when an employee moves beyond his or her comfort zone. As a matter of fact, the whole company is based on the idea of taking risks. As Alex has said, "We're a company that is willing to do new things." So, the way to get promoted at Benchmark is to, every so often, swing for the bleachers, knowing that an embarrassing strikeout may be the result. Then again, you might hit a game-winning home run.

Since I've always been a risk-taker, I value that trait in my employees. The fact is that you will never know how great your potential really is if you do not push the limits. Some of Laura

Neumann's experiences when she worked for Benchmark illustrate this point.

When Laura had her first performance review with us, she had been serving for some months as general manager of a private conference center in Racine, Wisconsin. She felt she was doing great work—and then I challenged her to think differently. I'll let Laura tell the story in her own words.

> *I was Benchmark's first female and youngest general manager and thought I was doing just fine. The center was doing well, and the owner had given me positive feedback, so I was feeling very pleased with myself. That is, until Burt gave me my first performance appraisal.*
>
> *I was sitting across the desk from him. On the desk, he had the performance appraisal form. As he talked to me, I kept trying to peek at the form to see what columns the check marks were in. I wanted them all to be in the "Excellent" column. Well, Burt noticed me doing this and that I wasn't paying any attention to what he was saying since I was so focused on seeing the check marks. So, he quietly put the form away, and I never saw it again.*
>
> *Instead, he said to me, 'Actually, Laura, I'm rather disappointed in you.'*
>
> *I was shocked. I couldn't believe what I had just heard. Then he continued.*
>
> *'I'm disappointed in you because you do everything well. You've never failed. How can you realize your true*

potential if you never run into a few brick walls? You're not going to be really good until you learn to take risks and learn from the consequences, good or bad.'

His message to me was that I couldn't just stay in my safe zone and continue doing what I had been doing because I was comfortable with it. I needed to stretch myself.

Well, I listened to his advice and acted on it and made a lot of mistakes along the way—some big, some small. I hired a limo to drive employees around north Jersey. That one didn't work out. I installed an innovative electronic key system for guest room doors. That didn't work out either. I could give you many more examples.

But another by-product of listening to Burt's advice was that I became the opening general manager of the AT&T Learning Center, a position that put me far ahead of most people my age on the career curve.

Let me add something to Laura's account. After the opening, the AT&T Learning Center was recognized as an exceptional operation. She later said that she finally understood my point: that we grow by entering that zone of discomfort, the taking-a-risk zone.

Of course, I would never have given her or anyone this advice if I didn't follow it myself. I've taken many risks over the years: some ended in success; some in failure.

One that ended in failure—but from which I learned a valuable lesson—involved deep-dish pizza. It was late 1974, and I was doing well as the director of operations at the Doral

Resort in Miami. And then some high-net-worth individuals approached me with an offer of a partnership in a start-up deep-dish pizza company. The first storefront was to be in Columbus, Ohio, which meant moving my family there. But the potential education and pay-off was huge: part ownership of a business that just might hit it big because it was a time when food franchises were going national. Dominos, Pizza Hut, and others were just getting started, and there was no successful deep-dish pizza franchise operation. It was an offer I felt I couldn't refuse.

I took this risk because the concept was good. What I hadn't taken into consideration was the fact that my new partners had no true plan of action for building this quick-service food business—and neither did I. In addition, what was a very serious business to me was secondary, and maybe even a pastime, to the capital partners.

Almost from day one, although the business was built on a great concept, long-term decisions were made for the wrong reasons. Quickly, the business started sliding toward a one and only storefront, and there was nothing I could do. The capital partners ruled. Though I worked hard, it was not enough to give me a positive view of the future. I may have brought my work ethic to the venture, but it was my partners who brought the money and made the decisions regarding growth strategy and selection of key managers. And they made decisions that I wouldn't have made—and didn't support. The direction I thought the business should take was lost in bad decisions.

In short, the risk I took didn't work out. I had made a career change into a business that did not totally fit my strengths or skills, and my partners could not help. As a result, I had to take

Taking Risks

a step I had never done before or since: I quit. Turning in my pizza apron, I went in search of new employment.

This misstep not only cost me time and money, it seriously inconvenienced Hermys and Kaira, who had to pull up stakes and move to Columbus. But in the long run, my deep-dish pizza work wasn't totally a loss because of the lesson it taught me: In addition to considering all the business factors, you have to consider the human ones. That was probably the first and the last time that I did not dig deep enough into what is actually the structure and relationship of a partnership and the alignment of goals among all stakeholders.

With my daughter, Kaira, in New York City when she was working on her doctorate.

Another example that comes to mind involves Scotty, that is, Scott McMinn, Benchmark's longest-serving employee. With Scotty, I took not just one risk, but two. The first was in hiring him. The Benchmark Management Company was in its infancy when I received Scotty's resume. At the time, Scotty was the food and beverage purchasing coordinator at the Waldorf Astoria Hotel in New York City—but he was also only 24 years old. Nevertheless, we invited him down for an interview. Afterward, I sent him back to New York with three of my business cards: one with the title of vice president on it; one with the title of general manager of The Woodlands Inn and Country Club; and one with the title of senior vice president of The Woodlands Corporation. Though Scotty was a little confused about who he was dealing with, he impressed me enough that I offered him the position of purchasing manager at The Woodlands.

Of course, by accepting this position at a fledgling company, a position that entailed a move to Houston, Scotty himself was taking a risk. But the risk paid off: Today, he is vice president of the Benchmark Equipment Company, which I set up at his suggestion—the second risk I took with him. In 30 years of operating that entity, it has paid off in $95 million worth of services rendered to our customers.

One of our general managers, let's call him John, brings us another example of a risk that he took about five or six years ago. One of the major expenses John had at the property he manages is the cost of electricity. His conference center is almost entirely operated by electricity, to the tune of between $300,000 and $400,000 a year. Over several years, this general manager had been working with a number of companies trying to buy electricity, using different contracts, fixed contracts, etc. Finally, one company promised that it could save the center seven percent off its electricity bill—and they put this promise in writing. John looked at the agreement carefully, he questioned them, he went back and forth, and he signed up with them. Then he got the first month's bill; it was 13 percent higher than all the previous months' bills. Then he received the next month's bill; again, it was 13 percent higher. And so it went—over several months.

John spent the next six months on the phone, making dozens of calls to the State Utilities Commissioner and the Better Business Bureau and anybody else he thought might help. Through all his efforts, he was not only able to get out of that contract but to get the money back that the company had overcharged the center. He described it as "a long and embarrassing struggle," but he succeeded. He had taken a risk—a well-thought-out one, true, but still a risk—and it did not pay off.

Risks can affect every level of a company—property, headquarters, even the whole system. One decision we made at the Home Office level directly impacted a new property. We had contracted with Deloitte US to assist in the development of and subsequent management of Deloitte University, their new leadership center in Dallas. It was obvious from the first that, despite the fact that it was an 800-guest-room facility with the capability to service up to 1,200 people a day, Deloitte was sharply focused on providing an unusually high level of personalized service. It was without a doubt their first priority.

As the team discussed how to deliver that service, they realized that they had an unusual situation on their hands. Hospitality people are often motivated by the tips that they earn. But this new facility was a non-tip environment. So the challenge was how to deliver outstanding customer service in that environment. From her experience at the AT&T Learning Center, Ellen Sinclair knew that the selection of employees was key.

So, she and her hiring team focused on just one factor: attitude. They selected individuals who wanted to serve and take care of people. Why was this a big risk? Out of more than 400 people hired to open the facility, 73 percent had no hospitality experience whatsoever. Most didn't know the difference between check-in and a dinner plate presentation. But it worked. The service at Deloitte University has been extolled as the best anyone has ever seen in the hospitality field. In fact, even some of Deloitte's executives have asked why they can't get our type of service in other hotel venues they use nationally.

A risk we took many years ago at the system-wide level was in agreeing to beta test the Delphi sales and marketing software tool created by Newmarket. This software has since become the product of choice for the hospitality industry; at least 80 percent of hotel companies now use it. But back in the late '80s, this wasn't the case. Delphi wanted to expand their existing product to provide hotel companies with not only software by location but at multiple locations and was looking for a company to test the software. Beta tests are very risky; if a client calls to book a conference or meeting and the software isn't working, the impression on the client can be very negative. Still, I agreed to let Benchmark be the beta site. As with everything, there were stops and starts and snags. At that time, people weren't as technologically astute as they are today. Certainly, there were crashes, and it took a lot of brain power by our employees to help Delphi build that multi-property edition so it worked effectively. But it was worth it because Delphi is a terrific tool, and we are still using it today.

Not long ago, we took a significant risk at the headquarters level. We not only brought in three of the highest, most important people at Benchmark from the outside; we brought them in over a short period of time. Giving three of the most important executive positions in this company to individuals who didn't "grow up" in Benchmark was risky, for sure.

But that risk was mitigated in my mind by two factors. Number one: They all had a history that was comparable to that of all the people who are successful within Benchmark; that is, they had divided their careers between independent operations that caused them to think on their feet and structured chain and franchise operations that forced them to follow a manual. All of us, including myself, had that mix of experience before we got to Benchmark. That was the first mitigating factor.

Number two was that they each came from a company that had an owner who was up to his neck in debt, had more problems than you could possibly imagine, and was very autocratic in his management style. So, from my perspective, all three of those individuals had already been in the worst professional situation they'd ever experienced in their lives, and each had learned a lot from the experience. You add those two factors and what do you get? A hiring risk but a well-thought-out one.

All of us who have been with Benchmark for several years know that we ran The World Trade Institute Conference Center for Pace University in One World Trade Center. And, fortunately, we also know that all of the employees and customers in the center at the time of the 9/11 attack escaped unharmed. What is not so well known, however, is that their escape was brought about by one of our employees taking a risk. When the planes hit the Twin Towers, the general manager and the director of operations weren't on site, so the sales manager was in charge. As it happened, a month before, he had taken an emergency response course the building held for all its tenants. One very specific instruction the tenants were given during that training was that the workers should not evacuate the building unless they were instructed to do so. But this manager took a risk and decided to follow his instincts. He instructed, and in some cases persuaded, everyone—employees and customers—to ignore that instruction and to go down the stairs (they were on the 55th floor of the North Tower) and get out of the building. He made the right decision. Had they stayed in the building, they might not have survived the catastrophe.

From the examples provided here, it is obvious, I believe, that we at Benchmark do not preoccupy ourselves with certainty of outcome in what we undertake. But I'd like to also point out that we have built the Benchmark culture and name on successes, not on risks that failed. Our clients pay us to get things right. Nevertheless, we do have a responsibility to them to try new ways, ideas, and approaches to the business. We also must have the wisdom to learn from both our successes and our failures. There will be times when any one of us will get it wrong. The secret is what we do afterward. As we pick ourselves up off the ground, we start the process of analysis. What went wrong? What did we miss? Why? If we do that, the risk that did not work out will also have a positive outcome: learning.

I believe that as we continue to follow this approach, Benchmark will remain a company that is dynamic and creative—and one where we accept the discomfort that sometimes comes with taking a risk.

Check Your Ego at the Door

Egotism is the art of seeing in yourself what others cannot see. -George V. Higgins

When I tell new managers that it is vital for them to check their ego at the door, I am not discouraging them from being proud of themselves and their work. Being self-confident and valuing your talents, skills, and accomplishments is a very good thing. But having an inflated ego is not.

A person with a big ego often has an exaggerated sense of self-importance. We have all heard someone boasting about something he or she has done or taking credit for an outcome that was really the result of a team effort. Since these people often exaggerate their accomplishments, I usually question the validity of what they say. It seems to me that bragging is often an attempt to compensate for some weakness. But such compensation doesn't work because big egos aren't just an irritant; they can be detrimental to the future of any business. Leaders with big egos can undermine a company because they are overly focused on how they are perceived rather than on the people around them and the business challenges at hand.

Being a successful leader does not require a big ego. Actually, it's the opposite. To be a good leader, you need to learn to be humble. Strong hospitality leaders understand that it is the hourly employees and supervisors who pay their salaries and make the business work. Strong leaders also know that you have to earn the right to lead—and that isn't done by bragging, posturing, and taking credit for the work of others.

When I was in the 4th ANGLICO, my Marine Corps Reserve unit, I learned an important lesson in how ego can be counterproductive. One of my last jobs as a sergeant was to prepare Marines who were about to go to Jump School at Fort Benning, Georgia. These Marines did small landing jumps, learning how to move their bodies, avoid injury, and understand the rigors of the School. During that week, those of us who had already been to Jump School suddenly received orders to participate in a separate survival exercise in the Everglades. We were divided into several teams, dropped

Preparing to jump as a Marine Reservist.

into the Everglades, and pursued by other Marines in airboats. The idea was to teach the men to handle the pressures and stresses of pursuit under very difficult conditions. Each team had 24 hours to get from Point A to Point B without being caught. I remember this exercise vividly because of the egos involved. Each sergeant was tasked with picking a team to take into the Everglades, and since each sergeant wanted, above all else, to have their team be the best, each jockeyed and maneuvered to get the best Marines on his team. Instead of focusing on the most vulnerable Marines' development, these few sergeants were all about winning and looking good.

Sensing what was happening, I decided to try to show my support for the "never-chosen" guys, who the other sergeants were labeling as "unproven." So I took the five most criticized Marines onto my team. A number of my fellow sergeants told me, "These guys will never make it through this exercise. It'll be too tough for them." They were wrong. Because I became one of them and did everything that they had to do—including breathing through a reed in the water to hide from the airboats pursuing us—we completed the exercise ahead of everyone else without losing a man. The supposedly five worst Marines got to Point B first. Because my guys knew I respected them and I assured them that they were up to the challenge, they responded with a positive attitude and determination. In short, I focused on the potential of these men who had volunteered to be Marines just like the rest of us.

Since any one of us can end up acting foolishly, it takes us to the key question of this chapter: "How do we avoid bringing too much ego to our workplace?"

First and foremost, those of us in leadership positions

have to avoid showing off or flaunting our position to our employees. For this reason, I try to arrive at a property the way everyone else does. One of the first times I visited The Heldrich Conference Center in New Jersey, the car service upgraded Alex and me from a sedan to a limo. Since it was too late to have them switch back to a sedan, we had the driver drop us off two blocks from the hotel. I did not want our employees, many of whom do not even own a car, see us arrive like VIPs.

If anyone in the world had the right to strut, it was George Mitchell. If you ran into him on the beach in Galveston wearing his fishing hat, you might end up in an hour-long conversation with him and never know he was a billionaire and the person who changed the entire economy of our nation by developing the now-famous "fracking" process in the oil and gas industry. George treated everybody the same. He talked to the gardener cutting the lawn in front of the hotel in the same way he talked to his stockholders. He was the one mentor who taught me the importance of checking your ego at the door.

A second feature of leaders who are appropriately humble is that they are willing to get their hands dirty. Good leaders, especially in our hospitality industry, are ready to do whatever job needs doing. They don't stand at a distance in a tough situation and bark orders at others. A case in point: During a stretch of 100-degree weather, the chiller went down at Cheyenne Mountain Resort. A group had reserved the entire resort and, naturally, were very upset because it was so hot in all the buildings and rooms. That left the Cheyenne Mountain team with the challenge of finding a way to make the temperature more bearable for their guests until a new chiller arrived.

And they did. First, they rented swamp coolers, a device

that blows air across water and cools the room through evaporation. And then one of the executive team members came up with the idea of duct taping the swamp cooler tubes and stretching them out into the hall so the cool air would be piped from room to room. While he did this, others passed out ice cream bars and cool drinks. The client saw the lengths to which the team was willing to go to do right by them and keep their meetings going until the new chillers arrived. But what's most important to me in this story is that the managers worked hand-in-hand with the hourly employees, forgetting all about their position as the boss; getting the job done was much more important.

Even more unusual is a situation that occurred during the opening of the AT&T Conference Center in New Jersey. It was what we call a "soft opening," when we ask a group of miscellaneous people—AT&T Group trainers, AT&T Executives, their spouses—to stay at the center and test the facilities and services. They would check in as guests to test all aspects of the operation. They would use the technology and phones, try the elevators, order room service, test the heat, sample the food and service in the restaurant. They would even participate in stressing the mechanical systems when in a coordinated effort, all the showers were turned on at once to see if the hot water supply was sufficient.

At 10 a.m., the general manager was in a meeting when the general contractor walked in and told her that if he didn't shut the water down right away, the center would not have running water for its first paying guests. Apparently, there was a serious problem with both the water pressure and the water temperature. The general manager thought, "Well, it's 10 o'clock;

surely everyone will have taken their shower by now." So she gave him permission to shut the water down and returned to her meeting.

The phone calls started immediately. As it turned out, not everyone had finished using the bathrooms. There were people caught mid-shower with soap all over them. But the decision couldn't be reversed; the water could not be turned on until the water pressure problem was fixed.

In an instant, the center's executive team went into action. One executive in particular, Jeff Farina, the center's then director of sales and marketing, personally delivered a huge cooler filled with warm water to a room on the fourth floor so the guest could wash the soap off. Since the cooler was full of water, it was really heavy, but Jeff not only got the cooler to the guest's room, but he managed to lift it above the shower rod—so he wouldn't embarrass the guest—and rinse him off.

Then there is Tony Costelli (at the time a food and beverage manager at The Villas of Grand Cypress) and his team, who got their hands dirty—literally—when, as members of a Home Office task force, they went to a property we had just acquired. When Tony and the team arrived, they found a demoralized kitchen staff and a kitchen that reflected it. Unfortunately, the team there wasn't responding to their suggestions for improvement. So, for seven straight days and even some nights, Tony and his team scrubbed floors and ceilings, deep cleaned storage rooms, repaired or threw out faulty equipment, and shampooed the rugs. It wasn't until after their seven-day housekeeping stint that they finally got around to doing what they had gone there to do: revamp the menu and reorganize the culinary operation. These managers certainly didn't let their egos get in their way. To quote one of them: "Don't divvy out responsibilities you're not willing to do yourself."

To me, what is often so exciting about the hospitality business is that you never know what each day will bring. Tony was certainly surprised by what he found and what needed to be done. These surprises are, in fact, "opportunities" for leaders to show what they are made of. You end up with a rag and a mop in front of you rather than an Excel spreadsheet. I have found that if you are comfortable with these kinds of scenarios, the business is fun and exciting.

Checking your ego at the door also means giving credit to others when that credit is due. One of the easiest ways to do this—which, paradoxically, is also the hardest for some people—is to let other people talk in meetings and during conference calls, asking them questions and letting them take the floor. One of our general managers ensures that this happens during conference calls by putting her phone on mute so she won't be tempted to interrupt or interject her opinion until the time is appropriate.

Ellen Sinclair, senior vice president at Benchmark, embodies a person who gives credit to others. It's what she did, for instance, when she led the Deloitte University development project and opening. After she oversaw every aspect of the creation of the unique service experience—implementing our unusual approach to staffing, inspiring staff with the right attitude to deliver personalized service, and putting in days analyzing potential problems and creating their solutions prior to opening—she focused on delivering several thank-you events for the employees who had worked to deliver the flawless opening. She wanted this done formally, that is, to give credit to employees and Deloitte's senior management in a group setting. There was no award or citation given to Ellen—she didn't want one. For her, it was all about all the other people with whom she worked.

Sometimes, professional humility can have surprising results. A few years back, we were one of six companies bidding to manage a beachfront resort. The whole management team, including me, spent all day making our presentation. The presentation was very interactive so that we could learn how we should tailor our services to the client's needs. As we talked about our slides, we all would add our thoughts to someone else's slides or answers to questions. At the end of the day, the group chose us to manage the project. We asked them what it was about our presentation that caused them to choose us. Their reply was that it was obvious that we worked together well and that there were no big egos on the team. The fact that one of our team corrected me on something I said stuck in their minds, leading them to conclude that we were not hung up on titles or corporate hierarchy.

Those of us at the Home Office also have to practice this principle by making sure that we empower the property teams to make their own decisions and do their work as they see necessary. A prime example can be seen in our approach to the TripAdvisor™ Business Listing program. The decision to use this program is made not in the Home Office, but at each property. About half of our properties use it and about half do not. They're the ones who decide if the program works for them. Clearly, those of us at the Home Office have a responsibility to trust our property teams and not let our egos get in their way.

This approach applies to the Benchmark brand, as well. At

each property, the name on the door is not Benchmark; rather, it is the owner's. We always put him or her first, so that our egos do not get in the way of his or her business success.

If we know ourselves well, know our strengths and limitations, we can more easily keep our egos in check. Here's how I think it works: Seeing yourself clearly enables you to accept the fact that you do not know it all nor can you do it all, which then allows you to turn to others for help, advice, support, and talent.

Fortunately, for all of us in the hospitality field, the work we are asked to do helps us to stay humble and grounded because every job in our business matters—and I have personally done almost all of them during my 50-plus years in the industry. Every day, in addition to our intense core work, we face dozens of challenges, many unexpected: equipment breaks down; a guest falls ill; 20 extra people show up for a banquet; a snowstorm strands conference attendees. Solving problem after problem, though, not only makes our jobs dynamic and interesting, but it also keeps us from taking ourselves too seriously. So maybe we're fortunate that the hospitality business itself helps all of us to check our ego at the door.

Let It Take Its Course

A lot of impulsive mistakes are made by people who simply aren't willing to stay bored a little longer. -Paul Aurandt

An important aspect of leadership we don't often talk about is knowing when to let things take their course. The natural tendency of most hard-driving managers and executives is to push forward for results, make something happen, or get to the finish line. All that makes sense. But the alternative approach is very important, too. The best outcome often results from being patient, slowing down the process, and waiting for solutions to surface on their own.

Let me start with an example that goes back to the mid-1980s when I was president of the International Association of Conference Centers. I visited Japan many times, speaking on the conference center concept to develop business relationships and establish IACC's first international chapter. During this time, with the assistance of my trusted colleague, Dr. David

Gottlieb, I learned to appreciate Japanese culture, their loyalty, friendship, and long-term views toward business relationships.

During my third speaking engagement in Japan, Ms. Kozue Honda, head of Human Factors, introduced herself to me, expressed her full understanding of the concept I was speaking about, and expressed an interest in introducing me to a client of hers. She was a strong woman and a leader in the Japanese business world, a rare accomplishment at that time.

After what seemed like a very long time, she introduced me to Mr. Nobuyasu Ishibashi, executive vice president of Daiwa House Industry Co., Ltd. (a world-renowned home-building company) and Mr. Hiromi Takagi, executive manager of TECH-R&DS Co, Ltd. (a Daiwa House subsidiary). They had an unusual interest in the conference center concept for Japan. We met at The Woodlands after several visits in Japan and, in May 1993, signed a letter of intent to form a joint venture for the establishment of Benchmark-Japan to develop and manage conference centers in that country. We also agreed to find a conference center in the United States they could purchase. They ultimately purchased Chaminade in Santa Cruz, California, and owned it for 10 years with Benchmark as its management partner. The property served as a case study for translating the concept into Japan and was an unusually successful operating venture.

Our mutual trust and loyalty allowed me to let our relationship take its course under the letter of intent without any of the business time line expectations that are common with a partnership agreement in the United States. I did not attempt to discuss a formal joint venture agreement right away until our growth and relationship strengthened. This decision was made in spite of the fact that our letter of intent included the following statement: "Within the framework of Japanese culture, it is Benchmark-Japan's intent to introduce, train, market, and manage in the US business-like fashion." We continued to operate with this letter of intent for 14 years until the joint venture was finalized in December of 2007.

Today, Benchmark-Japan (a joint venture between Ms. Kozue Honda and Mr. Hiromi Takagi and Benchmark Hospitality with Alex and me as representatives) has two conference centers in Tokyo: TCC Shinagawa and TCC Ariake. Future development plans call for a center opening in Nagoya in 2015 under a joint venture with several other Japanese corporations. During the window of time between 1993, when the letter of intent with Daiwa House was signed, until the joint venture was formally established in 2007, our partner changed from Daiwa House to Mr. Hiromi Takagi and Ms. Kozue Honda. Fortunately, allowing the letter of intent to take its course helped establish not only a partnership but a valuable relationship, one that remains strong to this day.

Hiromi Tagaki and Kozue Honda with Rita McClure and Alex (front row) and Greg Champion (back row, left) and Dennis Blyshak.

Another example of this principle is Chaminade. Before our Japanese partners bought the property in 1994, the original owners asked Benchmark to market the property while they continued to manage it. No matter how hard we tried to convince them that management and marketing had to go together because of our relationship with our clients, they insisted on managing the operation. The truth be told, at the time, Benchmark could have certainly used the income from this marketing-only contract. But we passed on the opportunity and let it take its course.

A few years later, when splitting management and marketing did not work out for Chaminade, they approached Benchmark for a full-service contract, which we negotiated and put into place. Our success at Chaminade came from our decision not to compromise our business principles and, therefore, not to push a deal before it was ready. Our patience has resulted in 25 years of success at the property with three different ownership groups.

Letting it take its course relates to almost every aspect of our business, including—which may be a surprise to some people—marketing. The marketing plan we developed for the Resort at Squaw Creek is a case in point. When this new ski resort opened in 1991, the First Gulf War had just begun, and the area around the resort had gotten no snow for two years. These two factors interfered significantly with the important process of establishing this new business. The owners understandably wanted us to discount rates to push revenue, especially for drive-in guests from the Sacramento area. However, we did not step away from our initial marketing positioning, knowing that we would be sending the wrong signal to the marketplace. This brand-new multimillion-dollar resort needed to "live" for 30 years. Discounting rates from the very beginning would undermine the following 20 years of value. Fortunately, I was able to convince everyone to be patient and let our marketing plan take its course. Neither the war nor the weather would be with us forever. Eventually, the resort's business made an upward trend—and with its reputation intact. As a result, the resort was able to maximize the appropriate rates and occupancy that the initial investment merited.

Most of the time, letting an issue take its course is a matter of timing. It can mean waiting to "pull the trigger" so that you do not make an important decision prematurely. There are times when we work on a problem or an opportunity without enough facts to make an informed decision. When that happens, there is a tendency to force an outcome, which really means basing a decision on conjecture or hope. Such impatience can be costly over an extended period of time.

Over the years, Benchmark has faced key business decisions for which we have never had adequate data or insight. We have been evaluating whether to establish a guest rewards point system similar to the ones major hotel chains provide for frequent guests. One argument was that such a program would help position Benchmark with certain demographic groups. Since we decided we did not have enough facts or historical comparisons to be sure the program would provide value to our property owners, we decided not to move forward. Simply put, we couldn't determine whether the costs incurred by the properties would lead to increases in occupancy and rate. And since, as I've mentioned before, Benchmark includes such an interesting and wide variety of properties, there would be a significant challenge in distributing the costs of a centralized program across all of our properties. Instead, we will shelve the idea until our research and data tell us that the return on investment clearly pencils out for the owners and the guests.

Even when we're talking about something as serious and important as the next major property at a new location, this principle applies. When trying to convince an owner to hire us as their management company, we do everything possible to paint the right picture for the owner, letting him or her know who we are and what we can do. Then, we just have to let it be. We can't force a decision; rather, we let it take its course.

This principle is so important to me because I have come to realize that decisions aren't made on a flat surface; they're made on a Rubik's Cube. You can keep turning one side of the cube, but as you do, the other side changes. At some point, you need to say, "It's not going to be perfect. The perfect can be the enemy of the good, so just let it take its course."

As our employees carry out their work at Benchmark, we know that they will exhibit the dynamic energy and enthusiasm that has been our hallmark for more than 30 years. But we would also like them to embrace the important role of patience and reflection. Once they have done their best, once they've invested their resources and talent, it's time to let things take their course. The fact is that if we continue to press, there is as much potential for things to go the wrong way as to go the right way. Letting things take their course just may be the way to go.

Unexpected Gestures

You can't live a perfect day without doing something for someone who will never be able to repay you. -John Wooden

In the world of business, all of us interact with a large number of good people, people who make a difference and make our work lives more enjoyable. But often, our lives are so busy and distracting that we cannot find time to show many of those special people how much we appreciate who they are and how they impact us. Early in my career, when I realized that this was the case, I began making small gestures to let these people know that I appreciate them as individuals.

These gestures most often take the form of a gift—large, small, and in between—and the recipient is usually a friend, a client, or a colleague who I think will appreciate my effort on his or her behalf. For instance, when I see a complimentary article about someone in a newspaper or magazine—the chairman of a company, a Benchmark employee, or a friend—I often have the masthead and the article matted and framed for them, knowing that, in most cases, it's something they would not do for themselves.

About 10 years ago, I took this step when Gerald Irons, whom I talk about later in this book, had a junior high school in The Woodlands named after him. There was an article in the local paper about the event, which I had framed and sent to him. Both Gerald and his wife, Myrna, sent notes to thank me, and I discovered that the article has been hanging in his office ever since.

I did something similar for Greg Champion shortly after he joined Benchmark as our chief operating officer. It was obvious that Greg was still somewhat uncomfortable because he had come from another company where there was a great deal of stress and conflict. Shortly after joining us, an article about him was published in a national hospitality magazine, so I had that framed and sent to him. It's now displayed in his office, a reflection of how much we value him in our company. And I did the same for John Chaney, former CEO of the company Pre Cash here in Houston and now on its board of directors. John is an individual who knows how to maximize the skills of those who work for him. We have dinner once a month, along with a group of other friends, and when an article appeared in the Houston Business Journal about him and his view of his industry, I had it framed for him. He was really surprised when the piece was delivered to his office, and he thanked me several times.

A friend of many years, John Deutsch, now retired, was a bank executive I met back in the '80s. I've always enjoyed doing things for John—framing articles, donating to his wife's charities, etc. Not long ago, Benchmark Hospitality hosted a dinner

Unexpected Gestures

at Sparks Steak House in New York, and we invited John. During dinner, he talked about how he wants to do another deal with our company before he retires. The last one he did with us was more than 20 years ago. A few days later, when discussing this business possibility, one of our headquarters executives said that he thought the gestures I had made over the years with John helped to create his desire to work with us. But as I explained, that was not why I did things for John. He is one of those people who do not get the recognition and appreciation they deserve, and I enjoy showing how much I appreciate all that he does for others and the fact that he is a trusted friend.

Of course, some of these gift-type gestures require more time and planning than others. A birthday gift I gave my mentor and friend George Mitchell is an example. Although for 30 years I sent George unique birthday presents, the most modest gift I ever gave him was the one he liked the most. It was a fishing hat with pins (like hooks) attached, each pin representing a part of his life. The first two pins were a tennis racket and a Texas A&M hat because George was captain of the tennis team there and served in the Corps of Cadets. The other pins commemorated many of the things he had done during his life: There was a Galveston pin, an oil rig pin, an environmental pin, a Woodlands pin—all kinds. It took me about a year to find them all. Though the gift was unassuming (the hat itself cost a few dollars), George thought it was the greatest thing in the world. Another birthday gift that George really appreciated was a mounted fish that sang when you clapped your hands. Corny, for sure. But it made George laugh, and he really appreciated it.

Making these gestures is also important to our business

partners—that is, our contractors, consultants, and vendors—because our success is so closely linked to the work they do. I think Alex's idea of whale tail carvings illustrates this well.

Alex had spearheaded the transition of a destination resort on Maui, which was completed in eight days and involved a lot of intense and difficult work. Our team of 27 handled the transition well—as did our industry partners, who supported us on everything from technology to sales and marketing to logo design. Once the transition was completed, Alex wanted to thank the whole team, including the vendors. So, we hired an artist in Maui to make wood carvings of the tail of the Alaskan humpback whale, a winter visitor to the waters near the resort. We then sent a carving to each of the team members and vendors who had helped make the transition so successful. We wanted the carving to be a reminder to each of them of their importance to us. Now, in addition to having the successful hotel conversion project on their resumes, they have a beautiful carving to commemorate it.

Wood carving of the tail of the Alaskan humpback whale.

Then there's Benchy, the teddy bear who sports a vest with the Benchmark logo. For years, we have sent a Benchy to anyone on our headquarters team and sometimes to others in the industry who have a baby. The importance of this small gesture was brought home to me when I received a thank you from a former Benchmark executive who had moved on to another company in order to reduce his travel schedule. Although he'd left Benchmark five years earlier, we found out that he had his first grandchild. So, of course, we sent him a Benchy with two sweaters—one with our logo and one without, so that if anyone from his present employer came by the house, he could choose to change out the logo'd sweater. He later told us that he really appreciated the gift, especially since no one in his new place of employment had acknowledged the birth of his grandchild.

Rikki Boparai, managing director for Personal Luxury Resorts & Hotels, Florida Collection, was another recipient of a special gesture. Here's what he said about it:

> *I was about to leave Cheyenne Mountain Resort to move to Bedford Springs for my first general manager job. My coworkers must have noticed that I had a couple of iron sculptures by a local artist on my desk because, when they presented me with my good-bye gift, it was a new sculpture by the same artist—this time, of a cowboy. That iron cowboy sits on my desk at home and is a constant reminder of my time at Cheyenne Mountain and the people I worked with, people who took the time and made the effort to commission a sculpture that would be very special to me.*

Rikki also pointed out a frequent gesture that Laura Neumann made when she was general manager at Cheyenne Mountain. Every time someone was appointed as a general manager, she would send that person a carved bear with the recipient's name on it and a message from her. This gesture took some effort on her part since the bear was carved out of wood, and to dedicate and sign it, she had to use a soldering iron—something she did herself each time.

I have been on the receiving end of such gestures, as well. Early on, when I was in college, I was in a battle with the university I attended over their requirement that I complete an entry-level internship program as part of my second year in college. Already an assistant manager at a hotel, I had enough hospitality experience for a college student. I was trying to get the university to trade that internship for another course that would be more useful to me—"Kitchen Design"—but I couldn't get the university to budge. That's when the then general manager of the Sheraton Four Ambassadors, a man for whom I had worked in the past, stepped in. He wrote a very long letter to the provost of the university on my behalf. (Keep in mind, I only worked for him as the front office assistant manager for a little over a year.) That gesture is something very few people, company heads or otherwise, would go out of their way to make. I've never forgotten his generosity and tenacity. His name is Larry Shupnick, now senior vice president of Interstate Hotels & Resorts, and this act of his enabled me to learn a great deal about kitchen design—as well as how I should behave toward others.

A second gesture that really meant a lot to me occurred in early 2000. American Airlines had interviewed a series of executives for their in-flight magazine. The question was, "If there was an item that you wanted that cost less than a thousand dollars but you wouldn't buy for yourself, what would that item be?" I was one of the 10 CEOs quoted in the article. Some of them said a bottle of 20-year-old Scotch; one said a pair of roller skates; and I said I would like a 9' 2" Hobie. Now, a 9' 2" Hobie was a surfboard made in the '60s, when I surfed in Florida. It's something I would never buy for

Unexpected Gestures

myself, one reason being I would never be able to stand on a surfboard today. However, Russ Bernard, the present head of Westport Capital, for whom we were running the Turtle Bay Resort at the time, read the article, had the 9' 2" Hobie made in Hawaii, and sent it to me. He didn't say a word; it just arrived one day. The surfboard now hangs in our office as a shining example of a gesture never to be forgotten.

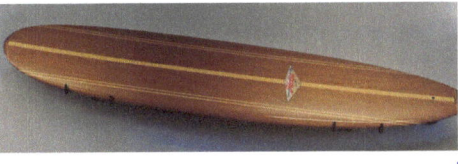
9'2" Hobie hanging on the wall in our Home Office.

    No matter where we are in life, we can all make small, meaningful gestures to those around us whom we admire and respect. But it's not as easy as it sounds. You have to notice what is going on in the other person's life and learn what really matters to him or her. The last example involves one of our senior executives. Over time, she noticed that a consultant with whom she had been working on a number of projects was always ordering grits at business breakfasts and even at dinners. So, one Christmas, she sent him a big metal basket full of packages of all kinds of yellow and white grits. The consultant told her he thinks of her kindness every time he serves eggs and grits to his family and friends.

    Let's face it: In our personal and business lives, it is not easy to find the time and energy to make these gestures of appreciation and recognition, no matter what their size. But knowing how much others appreciate them has always given me the incentive to make the effort. It helps build relationships—even friendships—and we never regret it.

    This is another one of my mother's lessons that I have never forgotten.

Can You Live with It for the Rest of Your Life?

There are some choices you can only make once. You can't go back to where you made a choice and then take the other one. -Mary Hoffman

We all know examples of companies that try something new. Sometimes the outcome is good. Southwest Airlines developed a whole new approach to boarding airplanes, and it has worked very well for them. Apple opened expensive, bright, modern stores with "geniuses" serving customers and set a new standard for the industry. But sometimes the outcome is not so good, even for great companies. Think of New Coke™. Or of Starbucks™ opening a slew of new stores, some right across the street from each other, then having to close thousands just a few years later.

A decision to do something new, to make a significant change to the way business is done, especially if it affects a lot of people or the financial health of a company, can be made hastily. Consider employee pension plans that companies and governments set up decades ago. As recently as 1998, 90 percent of Fortune 100 companies offered defined-benefit retirement plans to new employees. As it turned out, for many companies, these plans were unsustainable and became underfunded. Sadly, the companies can no longer continue with the decision they made years back. Employees at major companies, such as Macy's, Sysco, and Verizon, have been told that their benefits have to be frozen or cut back. Clearly, the leadership of these companies did not give enough thought to the long-term ramifications of their decision, or they would have developed different retirement plans.

The fact that companies often end up backing away from a major commitment made to their customers or employees is why I constantly ask our leadership team the question, "Can you live with it for the rest of your life?" whenever they suggest a new idea, initiative, or program. In the hospitality industry, there are many decisions to be made about such things as lobby design, valet parking location, the placement of the dishwasher room, and so forth that have significant long-term impacts on the business. For example, if the setup and location of a laundry room is inefficient, labor costs can be pushed higher not just for months, but for years and years. This same principle applies to amenities in the guest rooms. If you begin placing a special amenity in every guest room and then decide to stop doing it, you will end up disappointing and upsetting a lot of customers. Or suppose you decide to add an employee benefit that your competitors do not offer, and three years later, you realize it is too costly to continue the program and you have to stop it. Imagine how disappointed the employees will be.

Can You Live with It for the Rest of Your Life?

So you might be asking yourself why many businesses overlook this critical question before choosing a direction. Well, it seems to me that there are two reasons. First, they are too tactical and overly preoccupied with short-term outcomes or results, so they don't think strategically, that is, broadly and long term. Second, they don't really view themselves as a participant in their company forever and therefore don't mind that short-term decisions may have negative effects over the long haul. For example, a leader in maximizing revenue may opt to do something that will garner sales for the next five years, figuring, "Well, I'm only going to be here for a few more years, so someone else can deal with the problems later on."

Obviously, then, asking ourselves if we can live with a decision for the rest of our life improves the quality of decisions we make and creates fairness for others who follow us.

At Benchmark, we have established the habit of asking ourselves this question on many levels—and the results have usually been quite good. More than 10 years ago, we decided to change our approach to employee paid time off, moving from separate vacation and sick leave to total time off. An employee can now take off for things such as taking a child to a doctor's appointment or visiting a friend in the hospital. In short, employees can use their paid time off at their own discretion. But before we made this change, there was a lot of discussion; we asked ourselves again and again if we could live with this approach for years to come. We knew that once we made this change, we couldn't dial it back. Not only did we take our time answering that question, but we also took our time deciding how to transition to the new plan. Since the transition was not entirely smooth, we had to tweak the plan a bit to make it work.

But our thinking paid off, and we ended up in the right place, especially from an employee satisfaction perspective.

Another decision our company had to give very careful consideration to was whether to establish a national reservations center—an issue we have discussed for 22 years. The challenge was how Benchmark could give each owner the proper rate of return relative to the number of reservations they contributed to the system, which is why we never opened such a center until we finally devised a formula that allowed us to run a revenue support center instead. With this approach, we could create a fair system. If an owner received a little revenue, they paid very little, and if they received a lot of revenue, they paid a lot. This formula enabled us to open a revenue support center that we are prepared to live with in the long run.

As I mentioned in a previous chapter, early on in Benchmark's history, I asked this vital question when the Chaminade Resort opened and the first owners, the ones who built it, wanted to run it themselves and have Benchmark market it. At that point in the life of our company, we only had three properties and could have used the marketing fees the property would have given us—so it was tempting to accept the offer. But I asked myself, "Did I want Benchmark to market a property without controlling the quality of its operations?" My answer was no. I decided that we were never going to just market a property and then turn the customer over to someone else to serve them, no matter what the situation. I couldn't live with that approach over the long term, so I walked away from a tantalizing business offer.

Sometimes a business deal or arrangement only works over the long haul if the fundamentals are right. When we were

Can You Live with It for the Rest of Your Life?

asked to manage two properties, a golf course and a casino, in French Lick, Indiana, we spent a lot of time evaluating whether we, as a company, wanted to be affiliated with running a casino hotel. Our conclusion was that we did not. We explained to the owners that we felt that the facility should be positioned as a great destination resort that happened to include a casino rather than a casino that happened to include a hotel. Undoubtedly, the decision would make a huge difference in how these two assets would be marketed. Well, we started managing and marketing the property following our philosophy, but unfortunately, as soon as the economy became a little difficult, the owner changed his mind and turned French Lick into a casino that happened to have a hotel attached. We moved on.

As you would imagine, on a number of deals, my team and I have asked the right question yet still ended up with the wrong answer. A partnership we formed with Redstone Capital comes to mind. In what I thought was a reasonable step, we allowed Redstone to buy a portion of our company with the goal that Redstone would help to grow our company. As a capital investor, Redstone would invest in properties, and we would manage them. It seemed like a winning partnership; we had a lot of the same goals and values. This arrangement lasted seven years but, regrettably, nothing came of it as Redstone was not able to capitalize any projects. In the end, I repurchased the Benchmark shares. Though the Benchmark team went through all the machinations—the strategic discussions, checking all the boxes, and asking the can-we-live-with-it question—it did not work out. However, Redstone and Benchmark still retain a business relationship in considering future opportunities.

One commitment we have made relates to a simple but

important "gesture" that Benchmark makes for the Christmas holidays: the tradition of holiday cookies for the "Friends of Benchmark." When I was at The Woodlands, I began sending cookies to people who had, without any personal gain, helped me or the business in some way to thank them for their support and friendship. A few years back, when the company was going through tough economic times, we were brainstorming how to reduce expenses. Some of the team strongly recommended that we stop sending the holiday cookies. Though it may seem like the cookies and sending them would be a small expense, at the time, Benchmark's employees weren't receiving bonuses and we were cutting payroll. But I said no. Those cookies were being sent to people who supported Benchmark for years and even though it's just cookies, I want them to know how much we appreciate what they've done for us. This is a gesture I plan to make for the rest of my life.

Earlier in this chapter, I implied that "live with it the rest of our life" could, in fact, mean "live with it for a long time." And that's really my thought because, over time, as circumstances change, some practices have to

> **ALWAYS FAITHFUL**
> I must say I learned the importance and wisdom of this question the hard way. With just two credits short of graduating from high school, I joined the Marine Corps Reserve. I went into the Marine Corps intending to make it a career, but I joined in large part because of the legacy of my father, who was a military veteran in Cuba before Castro. That heritage and other emotional turmoil I was going through clouded my thinking. If I had asked myself if I was prepared to be in the military the rest of my life, I would have probably taken another course. Luckily, I had joined the Reserves and, after completing my active duty, was able to return to civilian life. For sure, serving in the Marine Corps was an enlightening, life-changing experience, which taught me a great deal about myself and the degree to which I could expand my physical and mental capabilities. From this experience, I learned the lesson being presented in this chapter and one I will not forget: Be careful about making decisions that you may have to live with for the rest of your life.

Can You Live with It for the Rest of Your Life?

be altered or even stopped all together. Since the company's inception, I had always read the performance reviews of every salaried manager and always sent a note to each person. It was an important and satisfying practice. I did this religiously until a couple of years ago when I realized that this practice was no longer tenable. When I started doing it, Benchmark had about 100 salaried managers; now, we have about 800. So, reluctantly, I had to stop sending the notes. In the same vein, I visited all of our properties at least once a year, but now we have 40 properties, so I can't do that any longer. Given what is on my schedule at the Home Office and with owners all around the country and the world, I must trust others to make these visits for me. Sometimes, you have to say good-bye to important practices. But I regret having to do so.

There are decisions we make that are done with the very best intentions yet still do not come out how we had hoped. At one of our conference centers, it was hard to find strong employees because there was no public transportation to the center. To address this challenge, the center team decided to use the van designated for taking guests to and from the airport to transport employees back and forth to a public transportation depot located about five miles away. This was a big help to our employees and enabled the center to retain good people. But this solution created another problem. The van was no longer available for transporting guests, which was its original purpose. If the center continued ferrying employees, the guests were going to be really inconvenienced. Obviously, the center couldn't afford to do that. What the team then realized was that there was not enough money available to purchase a second van. Thus, the property had started a program that it couldn't sustain. The potentially bad ending of this story was rewritten, however, by two industrious housekeeping employees, who started giving rides to their fellow employees in their own vans. But, in all honesty, that was just luck. The original decision to use the property's van simply was not well thought out.

It's sometimes very difficult to turn away from an idea or program in which the company has invested a lot of time and resources. In one such case, Benchmark had asked Tom Cupo and his team at The Chattanoogan to beta test PMI, a program used for more effective labor-cost analysis. We invested two years in testing this program, which represented valuable time, effort, and resources. But at the end of the day, we decided that the program was not going to save enough time and money to make it worthwhile in the long term, so, with great reluctance, we decided to drop the effort. What I always fear in these cases is that we will push on with a program just because we have already made a heavy commitment. It's an easy mistake to make. But, luckily, if we are willing to address this key question, we can avoid going down a road that will not improve our capabilities.

Many of us have read books on business success and leadership that point out how successful people and companies are those who have a clear and intense focus on their mission and who remain disciplined and steadfast in the face of distractions and changing economic conditions. In this chapter, I've tried to describe the one practice—in the form of a question—that has enabled Benchmark to stay on course and to avoid largely dead-end side roads that deplete our energy and our resources. In today's world, having this one practice is more important than ever as we grapple with the whirlwind of

Can You Live with It for the Rest of Your Life?

change and innovation that surrounds us in so many areas of business, such as customer service, marketing, and information technology. Of course, like every company operating in the twenty-first century, we have no choice but to be constantly considering new concepts, new programs, new approaches, and new processes and systems. But no company can do it all. As the ancient parable advises, we must be careful to separate the wheat from the chaff; otherwise, we may end up hurting our employees, our owners, and our company.

Thus, I recommend that anyone managing a business today pose this key question—"Can you live with it the rest of your life?"—to avoid as many false starts and dead-ends as possible. The alternative too often leads to undermining the trust and confidence others have for our products and services. With this one question, we can make it possible to come through, again and again, for all those who need us and depend on us.

Mosaic

One man can be a crucial ingredient on a team, but one man cannot make a team. -Kareem Abdul-Jabbar

Even though throughout this book, I have tried to make it clear that, at Benchmark, we all work together, there will be times when, as chairman, I need to make a decision on behalf of the group that furthers the capabilities of all the teams.

Such a time occurred just a few years ago. After doing

The mosaic that greets visitors to our Home Office.

some advance planning, one Saturday morning, I came to our offices with a few maintenance men and took the large Benchmark logo down from the wall behind the receptionist's desk. That logo had been there for more than 20 years, it being what everyone viewed first when entering the Home Office. Nevertheless, we took it down and, in its place, hung a work of art, a mosaic commissioned from Denise Liebl, a local Woodlands artist. As you would expect, there were a lot of questions about why I had replaced the company symbol at our front door with the mosaic. For me, the mosaic represents one of the fundamental strengths of Benchmark that has developed over time: The fact that, among our thousands of employees, we have available a tremendous range of skills and expertise. It represents our ability to reach throughout our organization and draw on that expertise, on those skills. It's this ability that helps to make us the dynamic, effective company we are today.

Look closely at that mosaic, and you'll see contemporary representations of various resorts and hotels, visual activities, plants, and landscapes. It's a visual way of showing how important everyone's performance is to the overall Benchmark picture. Each piece illustrates a person in our company who is not only very competent at the job he or she is doing, but also has other skills they earned from other places and times.

These skills are not geographically bound, nor are they tied to a person's title in the company. The most skilled person is always available to solve a matching problem. This commitment gives our business partners the best results possible.

What follows are a few examples of how the "Mosaic" of skills from the properties has been applied in our everyday operations to support the Home Office.

Today, many of our properties rely heavily on Micros Systems for managing their point-of-sale business. Micros is the one way our hotels can capture what items they're selling,

Mosaic

what prices they're charging, what inventory is needed. Though the system is very effective, many managers and line staff have difficulty learning and managing it.

As it turns out, Chris Steffich, then the food and beverage director at our Stonewall Resort and now in that position at Lockheed Martin Center for Leadership Excellence, had developed a talent for and an interest in databases in the Micros Systems. Since Micros is critical to handling our sales at the spas, restaurants, gift shops, and marinas, it's not an expertise you often see in a person like Chris, who is focused on food, cooking, and wine. But his skill has been of enormous help to Benchmark. Just recently, the company asked Chris to go from his property to one of our properties in Wyoming, where they needed a higher level of support for their Micros Systems. Chris supplied that support.

Chris not only trains managers and line staff in using the Micros Systems, he also helps build databases and cleans them up once they become too cluttered or unwieldy. He ensures that the system produces accurate and useful reports for our owners. And, ultimately, he helps our properties use the system to maximize staff productivity. In short, he is our Micros Systems one-stop guru. From his home base, Chris has traveled not only to Wyoming, but also to Hawaii, Florida, and other states for our company. He is a perfect example of the Benchmark "Mosaic" approach: getting the right person with the right skills to solve problems regardless of geography and job title.

One skill that came from an unexpected source had to do with trucking. We were faced with a number of challenges that arose when we were in the design and construction phases of a large hotel and conference center. The hotel was to be located in a suburban town, and town officials were concerned about the traffic that would be generated on the community's streets. To allay their fears, we had to provide a detailed report on how many delivery vehicles would access the site, along with their size, weight, and frequency. As we talked about this situation internally, we discovered that we had someone within Benchmark who was an expert in this area: Bob Zapatelli, our vice president of food and beverage. Bob was educated as a professional chef and food and beverage service operator, but for the four years he was in school, he had helped manage his family's trucking business and had actually driven the trucks. He knew the specifications—size, weight, load capacity—of every type of truck, from a semi-tractor trailer to a small panel van. This was certainly not the type of experience you would expect from Bob, but as has been the case so many times in the history of our company, here was an employee with an unexpected skill, a skill outside his known area of expertise, someone we could turn to for solving a problem.

So, Bob went to work with our team. He determined load volumes, volume requirements for pre-opening materials, for furniture, for equipment, for everything coming into the site, as well as the same information for ongoing operations—the delivery of foodstuffs, linens, and anything else that would be needed in the operation of a full-service hotel. His knowledge and skills enabled us to obtain the support of the town for the development of the property.

Then there was the loading dock challenge, another area where Bob's expertise came to the rescue. One of our hotel owners came to us for help in figuring out how they could overcome the delivery problems they were facing at their rather limited loading dock. The small size was causing backups, missteps, and other problems with the deliveries made to the hotel. Obviously, Benchmark does not have an employee whose title is something like "logistics analyst" or "delivery systems coordinator." But out of our "Mosaic," we could call on Bob again, who did a great job of reorganizing the property's loading dock and truck deliveries—and impressing the hotel's owners.

Sometimes, the skill needed is less concrete but real and valuable just the same. For example, there was a property on the East Coast run by a family who was a challenge to communicate with. For this reason, we needed someone with strong people skills, someone who could deal with these owners to ensure that we could properly do our job. Benchmark did, indeed, have such a person—but not on the East Coast. As a matter of fact, she was 2,000 miles away. But she was the right person for this unusual assignment. So we brought her in, she handled the situation as we knew she would, and the problem was solved. A typical chain hotel would not have taken this approach. They would have thought region, geography. At Benchmark, we think skills and expertise regardless of where they live, and that's what the "Mosaic" represents.

In addition to the advantage this approach has given us in terms of boundary-less support for some of the interesting projects we've taken on, there is another advantage: It encourages staff members to use the full spectrum of their knowledge and skills.

A case in point is Greg French, who was our vice president of golf. Whenever we operated a gift shop or other retail shop in any of our hotels, Greg was our go-to guy. As you would expect, he was an expert in golf course construction, design, and operation. But he was also a talented visual marketer from his pro shop experience. He organized and staged products that appealed to customers and gave them the ability to touch and interact with the products and encouraged them to make purchases. Greg was a significant asset whenever we were positioning one of our retail operations for profitability. It was a core skill in hospitality services operations that we did not have in our Home Office. Fortunately, Greg's talent and experience helped us make our retail design and operations profitable.

Since Benchmark is an international management company, we have created a Staff Support Group who work outside our offices in The Woodlands. They are very effective, solving all kinds of issues and problems for our properties. But we can't rely on those 15 or 20 people for everything. That's why we're constantly working to bring our "Mosaic" of skills to the highest level—so we take advantage of all those multi-talented, highly skilled people like Chris, Bob, and Greg. And in support of this goal, we are now computerizing the special skills and talents of several hundred Benchmark managers from all over the country, so when we have a specific request or challenge, we can quickly bring in the right person with the right skills to deal with it—no matter where they are geographically.

Ironically, another advantage of the "Mosaic" is that, in a way, it makes all of us a bit more humble. This is because one message the "Mosaic" sends is that we need to admit when we are not necessarily the best person to solve a problem. That attitude is very important. Harkening back to the "Check Your Ego at the Door" chapter, it's unfortunate when one of our managers or executives thinks he or she knows everything and can do whatever needs to be done. If that person resists calling on colleagues for help, he or she may let his or her ego get in the way of successfully solving a problem.

By calling on the right person, Benchmark gets the best result because we're setting aside ego and focusing on quality. The "Mosaic" and the hundreds of people in it make that possible.

I can sum up this philosophy with a little math: 1 + 1 = 3. Two people working together can equal more than the sum of 1 + 1. When you reach out to another person who has the skill you need, that person may improve whatever you're doing by perhaps one or two degrees. Over time, that turns into 15 degrees without much additional effort. Without a doubt, then, the beautiful mosaic that now hangs in the Home Office reception area represents our ability to draw on the skills and talents of all of our employees, no matter their job description or location.

Todo Se Puede

Nothing is impossible. The word itself says, 'I'm possible.' -Audrey Hepburn

My mother had a thousand challenges to face, but, in one sense, she had none because she believed *"todo se puede"* (everything is possible). This belief has seen her through many troubles and hardships and helped her overcome them. Finding an apartment for us to live in when my sister and I first arrived in this country was just one of the many challenges she faced as a young widow. In Miami at the time, 90 percent of the apartments did not allow children. But this did not stop my mother; she just kept looking until she found an apartment building that did. When she found it, she made sure that my sister and I dressed nicely when meeting the apartment manager so we would make a good impression. And she did all this without speaking English at a time when there were very few Spanish speakers in Miami Beach as the Cuban exodus was still a couple of years away.

Fortunately, my mother passed this attitude on to me and my sister, Maria Elena. But I've always wondered who had passed it on to her. Perhaps it was her father, who lived with us as we grew up. Here was a man whose wife had died young, leaving him with five children, the oldest being 12 at that time. Yet, he kept his family together and not only cared for all five, but also brought them up well. "If one of us has soup, we all have soup," was the way he put it. Interestingly, to different degrees, all his children have the same *todo se puede* attitude, with my mother having the largest dose. It was this attitude that enabled my mother to survive losing her husband, being exiled from Cuba, raising two children, finding a job in a foreign country when she did not know the language, and helping bring her two sisters, brother, and father to America. *Todo se puede* became her mantra. It was her way not only of surviving, but of enjoying what she did.

My grandfather with Maria and me.

This mantra was also her answer to all the hardships Maria and I faced. When we were struggling with the new language and a new school, she would simply say, *"Todo Se Puede."* What she was telling Maria and me was that with time, willingness, and effort, we could accomplish anything. And she was right, as mothers often are. Maria and I were able to adjust to our new country, learn English, and do well in school. And those words have stayed with us our whole lives. If you talk to my mother today, at age 90, she will still tell you, *"Todo Se Puede."* She might even add that the only things that kept her from being president of this country was that she didn't speak English and that she wasn't born here.

One outcome of having a mother with this attitude is that it encouraged me to stay positive and press on. When I think about how this attitude relates to company finances, I think of Dennis Blyshak. When Dennis was promoted to Benchmark's corporate controller, on his first day of work, he was shocked to find that there was only $1,000 in the company's cash account. But it wasn't the first time in my career that the coffers were low, even near empty. Many times, especially in the early years after I bought Benchmark, I had to sell things I owned, even dip into my children's college funds, to keep the company going. I once did that to support the company's health care plan and keep the employees covered with health insurance when things went upside down due to factors outside the company's control.

But to Dennis, $1,000 in the bank account of a company was like a dime in someone's pocket. To me, it felt like a million. Not to be flippant, but it just was not that big of a deal. I knew that when the time came for us to raise the money we needed, I would get it done. My mother had taught me that. In this case, I went to George Mitchell and asked him for a reprieve on paying my purchase loan from The Woodlands Corporation for one year. He agreed to add the payments to an 11th year of the 10-year loan. Fortunately, I never had to take George up on his offer because, over the following few weeks, we won a couple of management contracts, which enabled us to make the loan payment that month and every month thereafter for the 10-year term. Through that time and many others, I always thought things would work out. It was my mother speaking.

I am happy to say that Benchmark is full of employees who exemplify this attitude. Joli Furda is one. She started in housekeeping in a chain hotel, moved to a management position in a smaller hotel property in Alexandria, Virginia, and came to The Lansdowne Resort and Conference Center as an assistant executive housekeeper. Later, she moved on to become an executive housekeeper at two of our properties. But Joli wanted something a bit more and believed that it was possible to attain it. So, she applied for and got a job in Lansdowne's conference planning office, taking a pay cut in the process. In a short period of time, Joli became the senior planning manager, then director of conference services at Northland in Minneapolis, and eventually director of its food and beverage department. As with every other upward move she made, Joli rose to the occasion—so much so that it wasn't long before she became the general manager of the Capital One West Creek Conference Center we operate in Richmond, Virginia. She is still doing an outstanding job for us there—and now oversees Capital One's five conference centers, 11 fitness centers, and the Capital One University logistics, all because she believes that everything is possible.

Like Joli, Nate Waldron is a Benchmark employee whose belief that anything is possible has helped him succeed. Now director of operations at The Heldrich, Nate didn't start out in that position or even one close to it. Like me, he started working while in high school, in his case as a dishwasher. He continued working through high school, moving up the ranks to busboy to food runner to waiter to supervisor. By the time he graduated, he was the manager of an 80-seat restaurant in a local B&B. Then he branched out to larger properties, including Scanticon in Princeton, where he worked as a front desk clerk. It was while he was there that the training manager saw his potential and placed him in a two-year management training program. After completing that program, Nate went into sales, meeting planning, and conference floor management. As he continued taking on more responsibilities, he moved up, becoming the director of conference services at the AT&T Conference Center. And now he is a director of operations. Nate accomplished all this because he believed it was possible to move from dishwasher to director if he put in the time and effort to learn.

Both Joli and Nate have been with Benchmark for more than 15 years, so I've had the opportunity to watch their attitudes in action, attitudes that put and kept them on the road to success. I realize that among the more than 6,000 Benchmark employees, there are hundreds of Jolis and Nates, and I would love to talk about each of them, but for now, Joli and Nate must represent them. It would clearly take another book to cover them all.

I wrote earlier about Scott McMinn, an employee I've seen in action for more than 32 years. Scotty was 24 years old when I hired him as the purchasing manager of The Woodlands Resort and Conference Center. His first full-time job—he was just 17 and a week out of high school—was as a store clerk at a hotel in Rye Town, New York. His job description was, essentially, moving food in and out of the hotel's store room. But with his positive attitude, by 18, he was storeroom supervisor; by 19, he was a manager; and not too long after, he was food and beverage purchasing coordinator at the famous Waldorf Astoria in New York City. Today, Scotty is vice president of the Benchmark Equipment Company, our purchasing subsidiary. And after all these years with Benchmark, Scotty has to be a *todo se puede* kind of guy because every year, in October, we evaluate the savings made possible by the Benchmark Equipment Company to decide if we will continue with these services into the next year. If we ever conclude that the company's purchasing for our owners is not in their best interests, we would go to an outside service. But Scotty makes it happen year after year, even as his efforts and results remain under examination at all times. Of course, since he has never lost an ounce of energy or determination in all his years with Benchmark, his success comes as no surprise.

Though we have been discussing this attitude of anything is possible as it applies to individuals, the attitude applies to companies, as well. Even when I succeeded in buying this company in 1986—and believe me, it took a strong belief in *todo se puede* to buy a company when you have little money—there were many times when I had to remember my mother's counsel. One such time was in 1988 and involved our management contract with the Cheyenne Mountain Resort and Conference Center, at that time, one of five we managed. The owner, Gates Rubber and Tire Company, decided to consolidate all of its efforts into its core business and shed its real estate and other subsidiaries. As a result of that consolidation, Gates terminated our management contract and, along with that went the Cheyenne Mountain Resort, because when the new owners took over, they decided to use their own management company.

We did, however, receive a termination fee. And this was another time when Benchmark as a company had to believe in *todo se puede*. We decided to use the fee to carry Cheyenne Mountain's executive team until we could find them jobs elsewhere; that is, we continued to pay them a salary and benefits

Todo Se Puede

until such time as we could find them a permanent job. In some cases, this didn't happen until a year later. In the meantime, we would find things for them to do just to keep them working. For example, we would pay the salary of an executive chef even though we didn't have a permanent spot for him. When we temporarily needed a chef or sous chef at a property, we would send him and make up the differential between what the property paid him and what his salary had been at Cheyenne Mountain. We called these people the "boat people," the ones we kept on the boat until we found them a home.

It was a bold move. The hard truth was that keeping our people employed involved an act of faith since we had just lost a property that represented 35 percent of our company's revenue. But we believed that everything was possible and managed to pull it off, and those fine people we kept employed have played a big role in our success over the years.

A case in point is Merle Trammell, who was the director of human resources at Cheyenne and one of the people we carried. Merle eventually became our vice president of human resources. During her 20 years in that position, she helped us continue to keep managers "in the boat" until we found them a job if they lost their position in a

Merle receiving her "boat."

transition. And this is why, when Merle retired, we presented her with a carved wooden boat.

Our practice of continued employment is still active today. When we transition out of a property, we employ every manager who has received an acceptable performance review, and that includes those at the Pace University property on the 55th floor of the World Trade Center. After the tragedy in 2001, we helped Pace design and build another property in downtown Manhattan, one that we still manage for them today. But between the tragedy and the opening of the new property, any member of the World Trade Center Pace University team who wanted to stay with Benchmark could do so and did.

Just recently, we had to call on our *todo se puede* attitude when we stepped into the personal luxury segment of our business. Even though we were already managing eight luxury properties, we were taking a risk. We were concerned about how the marketplace would accept us in the luxury segment since our company's identity as a leader in the hotel and resort conference center segment was so well established. Then we bought MTM Luxury Lodging. By leveraging their reputation, hiring their key executives and adding their contracted properties, we were able to form Benchmark Personal Luxury Resorts and Hotels. It was a strategic risk not only because of the purchase, but also because we were positioning ourselves in another segment of the hospitality industry. A number of people told us politely that we were crazy. As a matter of fact, when we were attending the NYU Finance Conference right after the announcement, Alex had to spend the first 20 minutes responding to one observation: "I didn't know you guys were in the personal luxury business?" We knew it would take a while to get our clients used to the idea and that there was no guarantee that we would be successful in the new market. And there was the additional concern that we might water down our performance in the conference center business, on which we had built our reputation. Even some of our own managers wondered why we were diverting our attention away from what had brought us so much success to this day.

When asked why we were making this move, I had a simple answer: One of the main objectives of our company is to create opportunities for people to grow. And managing another segment in the hospitality industry creates an enormous number of opportunities for many of our employees, some of whom are recognized within personal luxury and have worked in that segment.

As an approach to business development, *todo se puede* doesn't always mean we are going to agree to just any deal or opportunity. What it means is that we won't end up dismissing possibilities and opportunities just because they are tough or challenging. The secret is to take on the challenge with optimism, realizing that though it may be difficult and may take determination, it is always possible.

Even though it was my mother who taught me my first lesson in *todo se puede*, over the years, others reinforced that lesson—people whose attitude that "everything is possible" have made a big impact on me. One was Estavan Zamoro, a Cuban-American and the resident manager of the Shelborne Hotel. He was the one who saw the promise in me and moved me from lifeguard to room clerk. Another is someone I mentioned in the "Unexpected Gestures" chapter: Gerald Irons. When he was in seventh grade, Gerald told his teacher and his classmates that he wanted to be a professional football player, a businessman, and a lawyer and that he wanted to get married and be a father. His teacher and his classmates laughed; his parents didn't. While they didn't use my mother's words, *todo se puede*, they gave Gerald the same advice in different words: They told him that he controlled his own destiny. And he did. Gerald became all the things he wanted to be and more. I met Gerald after I started Benchmark.

As I said, there were others who reinforced my mother's lesson. Among them are:

Mel Rose, who, when he was chief operating officer for Stouffer Hotels, hired me to help open its first resort hotel. I was an outsider at the time when Stouffer only promoted from within the company. Mel's willingness to stray from the norm later brought to Stouffer a great blend of outside management that added to the strength of the company and its future doubling in size.

Bill Friedman, the manager for whom I worked as a beach clean-up boy and lifeguard at The Shelborne Hotel. Bill was a plumber from Chicago who got tired of the weather there and became a pool manager in Miami Beach. Both as a boss and a friend, no one was more influential in my life during the ages of 15 through 20 than he was. His favorite expression was "press on."

Don Shula, who was an acquaintance rather than a friend. But his 17-0 season as coach of the Miami Dolphins was not without *todo se puede*. He managed and disciplined the team to great success with credit to all who played, and if there was favoritism, I never saw it in the games or at social events. Don was elected to the Football Hall of Fame in 1997.

Finally, Emilio Estafan, who was once quoted as saying, "I could have been a really sad person, but I convert everything negative in my life to a positive." Emilio and his wife, Gloria, have made an incredible impact on the Latin community worldwide. I was proud that he mentioned our relationship in his book. As a musician, entrepreneur, and music producer, I know he would say that *todo se puede* has paved the way.

Obviously, the *todo se puede* belief often encourages a person to take risks, which I talked about earlier. It is the belief that prompted my mother to take the risk of coming to the United States and to raise her children here.

It is this belief that enabled me to start my own company and enabled the individuals I mentioned among our Benchmark staff to establish outstanding careers. Finally, it is this belief that I hope all Benchmark employees will adopt so they can find all the success they desire and deserve.

Afterword

By Alex Cabañas, Chief Executive Officer,
Benchmark Hospitality International

"At the end of the day..." is a fairly common phrase, typically used as a discussion or a debate winds down. I have often heard these words from Burt and now use them myself. Once those six words are spoken, I do my best to tune out the noise around me and calm the thoughts swirling around in my head. Why? Because after "at the end of the day" usually lies insight, wisdom, and sensible solutions.

Burt and Alex.

You see, Burt has a natural ability to simplify the complicated. It is a trait he has exhibited all of his life and one I try to emulate. Fortunately for me, my career at the Boston Consulting Group helped enhance this skill through training and practice, but Burt comes by it naturally. Those of us who work closely with him know that, when you are wrestling with a complex issue, go see Burt and, within minutes, he will assess the problem, discuss the issues openly with you, and then say, "At the end of the day," followed by a simple and clear recommendation that makes you wonder, "Why didn't I think of that?" I have many memories of moments like these in my life.

In the fall of 1994, I had finished my first semester at Texas A&M University, and let's just say, I did not make the grades I was accustomed to making in high school. Disappointed and discouraged, I had to deliver the news to my parents. After delivering the message and explaining what I thought had gone wrong, Dad said, "At the end of the day, you learned in one semester all of the ways not to study." He was right. And from then on, every semester was better; in fact, I managed to graduate with honors. Many years later, in the fall of 2001, just over a year after joining the Boston Consulting Group, I was deciding whether to apply to business school. I had never seriously considered it before. But suddenly I realized that my career might require such education and training. I called up Dad, and, within a half hour, I rushed to send in my application. What did Dad say? "At the end of the day, you won't regret going through the application process regardless of the outcome, but you will regret not doing it." Though regret is not something Burt talks about very often, it was the perfect motivator.

Burt has always been adept at motivating those around

him. And the most characteristic way he has of doing this is through his *Burt-isms*. Unconventional and thought provoking, they create motivation and determination. Which is why I felt it was important for Burt to write down his ideas on leadership and some of those principles and insights that have been important to so many people. I may have even said to him, "At the end of the day, when you are no longer a physical presence at Benchmark, we must find a way to share your *Burt-isms* far and wide as the organization grows." Hence, this book and the presentation of principles that have guided us in the formative three decades of the company and its culture.

And so, to support this effort, I will do my best to share some of the "at the end of the day" takeaways that resonated strongly with me as I read this book:

At the end of the day...

...it is a privilege to serve the needs of others every day in hospitality.

...we should tune our hearts to "W.I.F.O." (What's In It For Others), and not "W.I.F.M." (What's In It For Me).

...we can rest at night knowing that we tried to make the world a better place by putting someone else's needs ahead of our own.

...simple human decency and kind gestures are appreciated by others much more than we realize.

...in hospitality, we make memories and emotions, not a

physical product, for a living. We would be wise to savor the memories and emotions we create for others.

…storytelling is critical to our culture. It opens the eyes and ears of our employees to possibilities and fills the soul with the good we do each day.

…self-worth is an emotional paycheck cashed in through random acts of kindness, and it is more important than net worth.

…we must have the courage to speak up and take risks, but also the humility to listen and adapt.

…each of us is responsible for protecting and nurturing our culture. Its future depends on all of us, not on a handful of executives in the Home Office.

…make a life in this business, not just a living.

Having laid out my list of takeaways from this book, it is vital now to turn to the wisdom of our employees, who, after all, are the ones who make this company what it is. In 2008, Benchmark embarked upon a strategic planning exercise focused on the next 30 years of the company. We even hired a very experienced outside consultant, conducted countless meetings, studied numerous books and articles on strategy, and on and on. Fortunately, as Burt noted in the "Listening Beats Talking" chapter, we had the good sense to take one additional step: We surveyed all of our employees, asking them two simple questions:

At the End of the Day...

What is it about your job that you love?

What about the job do you take home every day?

What we received back from the employees changed the trajectory of this exercise just by exposing the spirit of our company. The responses to these two simple questions revealed that our employees understood that it is all about the memories and the difference we make each day. That word "difference" kept appearing in the feedback we received: "I feel like I make a difference"; "I just want to make a difference"; and "I always feel good about the difference I made in the life of a person who's traveling and away from family and friends." So, at the end of the day, thanks to the wisdom of our employees, we were able to create our statement of mission and purpose, beginning with three simple words...

BE THE DIFFERENCE in the lives of our guests, employees, owners, industry partners, and communities. It is our common purpose!

Having finished this book, you will, I hope, remember this one guiding principle, flowing from the wisdom of Benchmark employees: "At the end of the day," they understand and appreciate what the hospitality industry is really all about.

www.ingramcontent.com/pod-product-compliance
Lightning Source LLC
Chambersburg PA
CBHW042336150426
43195CB00001B/5